A TASTE OF KASHMIR

GEETA SAMTANI

A TASTE OF
KASHMIR

GEETA SAMTANI

MEREHURST

Published in 1995 by Merehurst Ltd
Ferry House, 51-57 Lacy Road, Putney London SW15 1PR

Copyright © Geeta Samtani
ISBN 1 85391 474 6

A catalogue record for this book is available from the British Library.
The right of Geeta Samtani to be identified as the Author of this
Work has been asserted by her in accordance with the Copyright,
Designs and Patents Act 1988

Edited by **Val Barrett**
Designed by **Sara Kidd**
Photography by **Alan Marsh**
Styling by **Suzy Gittings**
Food for Photography by **Valerie Berry**
Cover Illustrations by **Ken Cox**

Colour separation by Global Colour, Malaysia

Printed in Singapore by Craftprint

ACKNOWLEDGEMENTS

In order to write a cookery book the ideas and recipes have to be shared with
family and friends, and without their help it would not have been possible to
complete this book.

My first and foremost acknowledgement is to my daughter, Ashwina, who took
great pains to help me with the research, compilation and typing of the manuscript and
for proof reading all the recipes.

Also thank you to my other daughter, Anita, for her support and encouragement.

I would like to thank Shanti Chopra, who resides in Delhi where she carries out her great
social work, and who kindly shared with me many of her recipes.

A big thank you to all the other contributors including Renu, Mr. Prem Sagar and his
wife Neelam and most importantly Massi Kailash.

Last but not least I thank my husband, Benny, for bearing with me and trying out all the
different recipes I cooked at home.

Previous pages: Emperors Kashmiri Biryani and aubergine pickle.

CONTENTS

INTRODUCTION

Once upon a time there was a vast lake plagued by a water demon. The goddess Parvati, wife of the King-God Shiva, saddened by this infestation in her favourite playground, cracked an opening in the mountainous wall surrounding the lake. All the water was drained out together with the dreaded demon. There remained a beautiful, green and fertile plateau, 1,800metres (6,000 feet) above sea level, filled with majestic rivers and lakes. Thus was created the earthly paradise of the Vale of Kashmir.

A turbulent history of mighty warlords; a mélange of cultures; extreme seasons; a distinctive, almost nomadic way of life; all these have allowed Kashmir to develop an effervescent niche in the Asian continent.

Today, Kashmir is the home not only to the Hindus and Muslims, but because of its proximity to Tibet and China, it also accommodates a population of Buddhists. As well as this, Kashmir has had a continual succession of Kings - the Afghans, the Moguls, the Sikhs and even the Britons, at one time or another have tasted the fruits of Kashmir and indeed they have not left the land untarnished. They have moulded the land and textured it with their own individual culinary and cultural whims. Thus remains a land whose cuisine and environment have been enticingly peppered with the wares and traditions of settlers long gone. It is from these influences and the agricultural patterns of the land that Kashmiri cooking has been derived.

Rice crops make a mosaic across the land bringing a plushness of colours - the bright emerald green in summer to the pure golden shades in Autumn, just before harvesting. Even today, in times of modern technology, farmers and their families work side by side to gather their crops. It is here on the fields that salt tea is served in abundance. A special leaf is boiled together with water, milk, salt, and cooking soda until an almost pink colour permeates through the tea. The tea is then poured into wooden bowls and is fervently drunk by all.

Wheat is also grown in Kashmir, and it has an important role in the region's cuisine. Kashmiri bread is among the best in the world. There is nothing like sitting by a warm fire with Qahwa (Kashmiri tea) and a slice of Sheermal (an almost biscuit-like bread).

Vegetables such as turnips, radishes, and morels are grown in excess alongside orchards of almond, apple, peach and plum trees. The intense flavours found in most of these foods add exquisite tastes to Kashmiri cuisine, unsurpassed by other Indian delights.

The still waters of Kashmir are blanketed with a vigorous display of pink water lilies underneath which lies an artichoke-like vegetable called lotus root. This is used in many Kashmiri dishes, as an accompaniment to meat or fish or even cooked and served on its own.

Floating vegetable gardens occupy Kashmir's lakes. They are built using layers of water reeds, lake weeds and mud to form a 13-15cm (5-6 inch) high island, on which watermelons, cucumbers, tomatoes, radishes, herbs and greens grow aplenty. These fruits and vegetables are then carefully picked by the beautiful women of Kashmir adorned in their pherens (Kashmiri outfit). Indeed, these women are masters at cutting and collecting the fruits and vegetables and are themselves the keepers of the most enticing secrets of Kashmiri cuisine. Fruits and vegetables from the floating green-grocers are transported to the travelling vegetable markets. These make their way from houseboat to houseboat, supplying fresh produce to all households early every morning.

Mustard oil is used a great deal for cooking in Kashmir, and in spring the fields of yellow mustard are a golden blaze against the backdrop of blue skies and snow-covered mountain peaks. The Vale of Kashmir becomes a colourful patchwork of crops, trees and rivers. As the seasons change the colours intensify from spring green to winter rust.

A treasure among flowers, the saffron-producing crocus, grows profusely in Kashmir. These virtual jewels are found tucked away in even the most impoverished of households. Mauve blankets of the crocus sativus plant cover the fields of Pampore by mid-October. This district has become a tourist spot, with cars full of travellers viewing with wonder the magical splendour before them.

The most colourful event in a Kashmiri Muslim's calendar, is the celebration banquet or Wazawaan. Special chefs (wazas) are called in to prepare sumptuous banquets over-flowing with meats and sweetmeats. The celebration begins with the procession of the wazas and a group of sheep on their way to be slaughtered. The head waza beheads the sheep in a sacrificial ceremony and the sheep are then cut up into pieces.

The skill or art of the wazas is not taught in a formal way, but is simply passed down from father to son. It does not comprise solely of recipes or culinary techniques, as a good waza is learned in butchery and even herbal gardening. The spices used by the waza are a closely guarded secret and have remained unchanged over the centuries. The head waza supervises the cooking and adds generous amounts of cardamom, cinnamon, red pepper powder, turmeric and crushed aniseed. He haphazardly throws the spices into the huge cooking pots, arranged on blazing log fires, using the age-old technique of the finest Indian chefs, 'andaaz'. Andaaz is a technique that is developed through experience or a keen eye for cooking. Literally it means 'to approximate the quantity required', and this ability shows the emotional link between a cook and his cuisine. Indeed, it is a seasoned cook who can extract the most delicious flavours using no measurements, but only good judgment.

Wazawaan feasts are always eaten off a large platter serving approximately four. Men and women sit separately, as is common Islamic practice. However, the most endearing feature in Kashmiri society, is that both rich and poor guests are invited to share the same platter of food.

Cashmere wool, the hand-woven carpets, exquisite shawls, the remarkable beauty of the Kashmiri people and of course the formidable cuisine, continue to brand Kashmir an Elysian paradise and truly a 'land of milk and honey'.

Easy Route to Confident Kashmiri Cooking

Kashmiri cuisine is very rich and has an almost regal quality to it. An assortment of nuts, cream, yogurt, milk, saffron and aromatic spices are combined to produce an array of culinary delights.

It is the Kashmiri red chillies that add not only flavour but also colour to the cuisine. These chillies are not overpoweringly hot, but have a more subtle, delicate flavour. Unfortunately they are not always available in the UK. However, I have found that a combination of ground dried red chillies and a good paprika is just as effective - giving not only flavour but also that brilliant red colour. Remember chillies are a personal taste, so do not be afraid to alter the amount of chilli in any of the recipes according to your own palate.

As far as it is possible, I suggest that you grind your own spices. Buy them in their whole form and grind them in a coffee grinder. The freshly ground powders can then be stored in an airtight container so as to retain the flavours and the piquant aromas. If this is not possible the spices can be purchased ready-ground. Although garam masala (a mixture of spices) is available ready-made, it is worth grinding this yourself to suit your own taste. Each region, and indeed even each household, in India uses their own particular blend of spices to prepare this vital culinary ingredient. Especially when preparing Kashmiri cuisine it is important to try and use the Kashmiri garam masala (see page 9).

In many of the recipes you will notice that I have used ground fresh ginger and garlic. Both for convenience and to save time, it is a good idea to purée large quantities of ginger and garlic, separately, in a blender or food processor. Store in airtight containers in your fridge or freezer.

At an Indian dining table, food is rarely portioned out and you will often find a selection of dishes adorning the table. Everyone helps themselves and so you will find that a dish that serves 4 will often stretch, with various accompaniments, to serve 8.

Kashmiris are very fond of mustard oil and use it in almost every dish. The mustard oil gives their cuisine its own unique flavour. Try to use mustard oil at first and then, if you prefer, you can substitute any other oil of your choosing. If you find that there is excess oil in the dish before serving, simply spoon it out. If you don't mind the oil, then dip in a piece of Kashmiri bread for a delicious treat. Also remember that when preparing this cuisine, Indians season their food lavishly with a variety of whole spices; these spices are not to be eaten and should be removed while eating.

Most dishes can be frozen and then defrosted in the fridge, slowly and thoroughly before gently reheating. As freezing often thickens sauce-based dishes, you may find that adding a small amount of water, as required, will restore the dish to its initial splendour. Many of the sauce-based dishes can be successfully reheated in the microwave.

Cooking Utensils

No special utensils are required for Kashmiri cooking.

Although not essential, I have found that a cast-iron karahai is very useful as it can be used for both cooking and deep-frying. A karahai is a round-bottomed pan with two handles, very similar to a Chinese wok. Cooking meat and some vegetables in a karahai gives the food an extraordinarily delightful flavour.

A heavy-based pan is an important utensil in every kitchen as it cooks the food evenly and gently. Make sure you have tight-fitting lids, as much of the cooking is done covered to ensure that the liquid does not evaporate too quickly; extremely useful when preparing rice.

A non-stick frying pan is useful for quick-frying. A tawa, (a heavy, flat pan), is essential for cooking excellent chapattis or any Indian bread. It is made of cast-iron and is traditionally heated on coal fires. Modern tawas heat on normal gas or electric cookers. In the UK a griddle is easily available and just as effective. However a tawa is obtainable from any Indian shop.

Special Fresh Ingredients

Garam Masala

There are many variations of garam masala and each home has their own special blend handed down through the generations. Garam masala is generally added to most dishes just before serving, to impart that authentic taste and aromatic fragrance. Below I have given a recipe for garam masala which you may typically find in any Kashmiri home, although each home would probably have their own slight variation.

To make 250g (8 oz) garam masala:

30g (1 oz) black cummin seeds
125g (4 oz) brown cardamom pods
30g (1 oz) whole black peppercorns
30g (1 oz) cinnamon sticks
30g (1 oz) whole cloves
12 blades mace
2 whole nutmegs

1. Dry roast all the spices, except the nutmeg, in a heavy-based pan on a very low heat until a strong aroma is released. Allow to cool.
2. Grind all the roasted spices together in a coffee grinder.
3. Grate the nutmeg and add it to the ground spice mixture.
4. Store in an airtight container.

Paneer

Although paneer is available from some Asian shops I prefer to make my own. Paneer can be used in savoury dishes and for making sweets.

To make approx. 250-350g (8-12 oz) of paneer:
1 litre (32 fl oz) full cream milk
2-3 tablespoons lime juice
250ml (8 fl oz) natural yogurt (optional)

1. Heat the milk in a pan and bring to the boil. Stir continuously to prevent it from sticking to the bottom and to prevent cream forming on the top. When it comes to the boil, reduce the heat.
2. Add 2-3 tablespoons lime juice or mix 1-2 tablespoons lime juice with the yogurt and add to the boiling milk. When the milk curdles remove the pan from the heat.
3. The whey (water) from the paneer should be green in colour, if not, add a little more lime juice. Leave for 20 minutes.
4. Place a muslin cloth in a colander set over a bowl and strain the paneer.
5. The whey from the paneer can be used to make excellent gravies and soups.
6. To make pressed paneer, leave it in the muslin and press it down with a heavy weight for at least 2 - 3 hours. This can then be cut up as desired.

Suitable for freezing.

Khoya (Condensed Milk)
Khoya is also called Mawa and can be used for both savoury and sweet dishes.

To make Khoya from milk:
1. Boil 1 litre (32 fl oz) full cream milk in a heavy-based pan on medium heat. Stir continuously to make sure that the milk does not stick to the bottom of the pan.
2. Boil gently until all the moisture evaporates and the consistency of the Khoya is similar to a soft, sticky dough. Use as required.

Suitable for freezing.

Mustard Oil (Sarson Ka Tel)
Kashmir is known for its wonderful fields of golden mustard. The oil is made from the mustard seeds and is pungent in its raw form. However, on heating the pungency is eliminated and a sweet flavour remains. It is an important oil in Indian cuisine, particularly for making pickles. In Kashmir it is also used for everyday cooking. I have used mustard oil in most of my recipes, to add to the flavour of the dishes, but any other oil can be used instead.
Before using mustard oil, heat it to smoking point (to eliminate the pungency), lower the heat and simmer for a few seconds. The oil is now ready for use.

Glossary

Aniseed (Saunf): Aromatic and sweet-flavoured seeds of the anise plant. Aniseed is an important spice in Kashmiri cuisine. It is used in savoury dishes and for flavouring drinks, and is also eaten after meals to aid digestion.

Asafoetida (Hing): This is the dried resinous gum of a plant grown in Afghanistan and Iran. It is used sparingly as it has a very strong flavour. Kashmiri Brahmins religiously forego onions and garlic, substituting asafoetida to flavour their dishes. Asafoetida can be bought ground or in pieces.

Atta or Chapatti flour: Very fine wholewheat flour used to make a variety of breads and rotis.

Bitter Gourd (Karela): A long green vegetable with a coarse surface, it has a bitter flavour and is often thought to be a delicacy. Available from Asian grocers.

Black whole lentils (Mah Ki Dal): Black, silky and round, this lentil requires a minimum of 4-5 hours soaking before use. It is also extremely wholesome and nutritious.

Cardamom Pods (Elachi): There are three types of cardamom, the small green type (Choti Elachi), the brown type (Badi Elachi), and finally the third variety are bleached white cardamoms. Green cardamom pods are the most commonly used and have a more mellow flavour, they are also aromatic. The brown cardamoms have a coarser skin and a more pungent flavour.

Carum Seeds (Ajwain): From the same family as caraway and cummin, it tastes similar to thyme. Generally used in curries or batter mixtures for frying fish, chicken or vegetables.

Chillies (Mirchi): Grown all over India, chillies are found in most Indian meals. They vary in shape, colour, size and strength. It is very difficult to judge the hotness of a chilli but as a guide the fatter the chilli the less pungent it is likely to be. The seeds of the chilli are the hottest part, so for a milder flavour it is advisable to remove the seeds before adding the chilli to your dish.

Cummin - Black (Shahjeera): These are the black seeds of the cummin plant. Their flavour is more intense than the white variety. These seeds are used liberally in Mughlai cooking and pickling.

Cummin - White (Jeera): These seeds are more commonly used and are indispensable in the preparation of most curries. Cummin seeds have a heavy, distinctive aroma, are stronger than caraway seeds and have a mild after-taste of anise.

Dried Red Chillies (Lal Mirch): The ripened green chillies in time turn red. These are then dried, changing the texture and flavour. The dried chillies are often ground to a fine powder for convenient use in cooking. Kashmiri red chillies are milder in strength and sweeter tasting than other types and it is their bright red colour that brings life to the most lacklustre dish.

Fenugreek Leaves (Mehti): This green leaf has a bitter but piquant flavour. It tastes especially good with meat or fish curry and once the leaf is cooked an enticing aroma is released. The fresh leaves are cooked as a vegetable and the dried leaves are used for flavouring.

Fenugreek Seeds (Mehti Dana): Small, yellow seeds with a characteristically bitter flavour. Their dormant flavours become more pronounced once the seeds are fried.

Garam Masala: a blend of spices. (See page 9.)

Ghee: Made from clarified butter and widely used in Kashmiri cuisine.

Ginger, dried (Sounth): Dried ginger can be used whole or ground and has a slightly different flavour to fresh ginger.

Ginger, fresh root (Adrak): Fresh root ginger has an aromatic, sharp flavour that gives zest to most dishes and even to drinks. It can be puréed and stored in the fridge or freezer.

Gram Flour (Besan): This flour is made from ground split yellow chick-peas (channa) and is available from most Asian grocers.

Jaggery (Gur): A form of raw sugar, honey-brown in colour. It comes in solid blocks and is available from most Asian shops.

Kewda Water (Kewda Ruh): Obtained from the flower of the kewda plant, it is used to flavour sweets and some savoury dishes. Available from Asian grocers.

Lotus Root (Nadhru or Bhein): Lotus roots grow in the still waters of Kashmir, underneath the lovely lotus flower. Brown in colour, the lotus root vegetable resembles a flute and tastes similar to artichokes. The seeds of the lotus flower are also a delicacy.

Mace and nutmeg: Mace and nutmeg are two different spices produced from the same tree. Nutmeg is used in Indian curries and as a spice in garam masala. It is also used to flavour sauces and sweets. Nutmeg is used finely grated whilst mace is coarsely crushed.

Mango, dried (Amchoor): Raw mangos are dried and used as a souring agent in cooking. Can be bought whole or powdered.

Nigella (Kalonji): Small black seeds similar to onion seeds.

Paneer: Home-made cheese. (See page 9.)

Paprika: Paprika is made from dried sweet pepper found in Hungary and Spain. Indian paprika is made from a mild chilli pepper known as Deghi Mirchi, grown in Kashmir. It lends a brilliant red colour to the dish without making it too peppery hot.

Pomegranate Seeds (Anardhana): These are the dried seeds of the pomegranate fruit. They add a tangy flavour to any dish.

Poppy Seeds (Khus Khus): Poppy seeds come from the poppy plant. They are used to thicken and enrich curries and sauces. They are commonly ground, or roasted and then ground, adding a nutty flavour to cooking. Generally, white poppy seeds are used in Indian cuisine.

Rose Water (Gulabjal): This is a special strain of rose which is cultivated solely for culinary purposes. The petals of the flower are used for garnishing rich Moghlai dishes and the rose essence is extracted for use in desserts and some savoury dishes. It is this essence which is diluted to make rose water. The rose petals are also cooked with sugar to make Gulkand, a sweet which carries digestive and medicinal properties.

Saffron (Kesar): One of the world's most expensive spices, saffron is an aristocrat with its subtle aroma and reddish-gold colour. Kashmir, Iran and Spain are the principal growers of saffron. Saffron is a luxurious treat used in Kashmiri cuisine, especially on festive occasions.

Silver Leaf (Vark): Real silver is beaten continuously until it forms a thin leaf-like form. It is only then that the silver is edible. Silver Leaf is used widely in Indian cuisine for decoration. Gold was also beaten in a similar way to form gold leaf, however due to the expense the use of gold leaf for garnishing is increasingly diminishing. Silver leaf is available at selected Asian grocers.

Tamarind (Imli): Dried pods of the tamarind tree are used to give a sourish taste to Indian dishes. Tamarind is available in blocks or in a paste form.

Turmeric (Haldi): Turmeric is a deep yellow colour and is used as both a condiment and a natural dye. It is said to have healing properties and generally only a small amount is added during cooking to give that typically yellow-orange Indian colour. Available in whole or ground form.

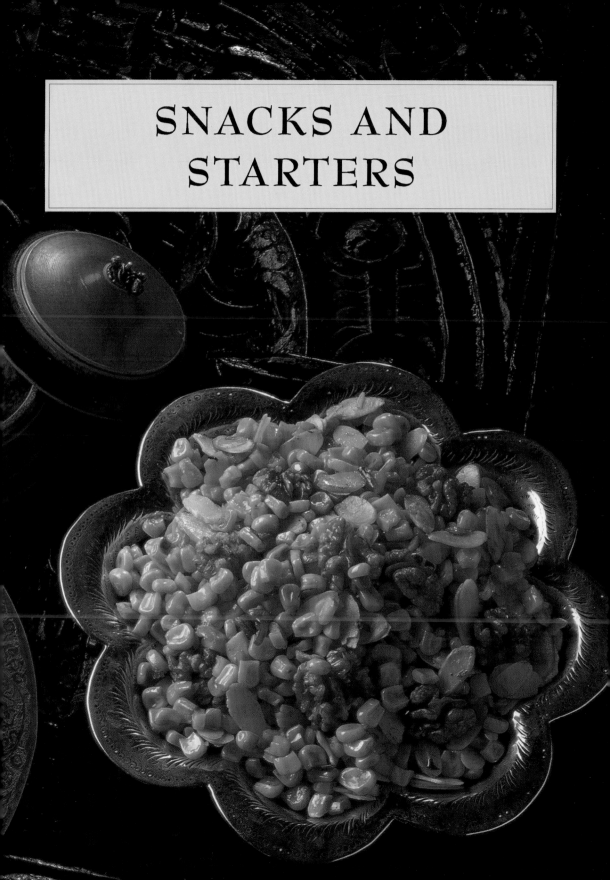

SNACKS AND STARTERS

Gosht Ki Dahi Bare
(Meat Dumplings in Yogurt)
SERVES 6

*T*hroughout the rest of India Dahi Bares are vegetarian and are made with lentils and yogurt. Kashmiris in their enthusiasm for meat have altered this Indian national dish and use meat instead of the usual lentil dumplings resulting in an exquisite delicacy.

500g (1 lb) lamb or beef mince

8 tablespoons fresh bread crumbs

1 teaspoon ground turmeric

1 teaspoon garam masala

1 teaspoon puréed or grated fresh root ginger

1 teaspoon puréed or minced garlic

1 tablespoon fresh mint leaves, chopped

salt to taste

oil for shallow frying

375ml (12 fl oz) natural yogurt

$1/2$ teaspoon chilli powder

3-4 tablespoons fresh coriander leaves, finely chopped

$1/2$ teaspoon aniseed, roasted and crushed

Preparation time: 20-30 minutes

Cooking time: 20-30 minutes

1. Put the meat and breadcrumbs into a bowl and knead well together.
2. Add the turmeric, garam masala, ginger and garlic pastes, mint and salt to taste. Mix well.
3. Shape the mixture into cutlets.
4. Fry them in hot oil until golden brown and cooked through. Remove and keep warm.
5. Beat the yogurt until creamy Add salt to taste.
6. Arrange the Dahi Bares on a serving dish and pour the yogurt over them.
7. Sprinkle with the chilli powder, fresh coriander and crushed aniseed.

Serve as a light snack or with any main meal.

Unsuitable for freezing.

Previous pages: Gosht Ki Dahi Bare, Besan Macchi (p.17) and Kashmiri Makki Akroat (p.21).

Besan Macchi
(Fish Fritters)
SERVES 4

*K*ashmir has a vast number of grandiose lakes and all Kashmiri fish comes from *them. You can use any soft flesh fish in this recipe.*

4 cloves garlic, peeled
2.5cm (1 inch) piece fresh root ginger, peeled
1 teaspoon chilli powder
3 tablespoons fresh coriander leaves
3 tablespoons mint leaves
2 tablespoons lemon juice
3 tablespoons gram (chick-pea) flour
salt to taste
500g (1 lb) fish, coley or sole fillets, skinned and cut in 5cm (2 inch) pieces
mustard oil for frying

Preparation time: 1 hour 45 minutes
Cooking time: 30 minutes

1. Put the garlic, ginger, chilli powder, coriander leaves, mint leaves and lemon juice into a blender and process well.
2. Put the gram flour, the blended mixture and salt to taste into a bowl and mix to a paste. Spread the mixture over the fish and leave in a cool place to marinate for 1 hour.
3. In a deep pan heat the mustard oil until smoking hot. Lower the heat until the smoke disappears as this eliminates the pungency of the oil and gives it a sweeter taste. Fry the marinated fish until golden brown.

Serve with Akroat Pudina Chutney.

Unsuitable for freezing.

Akroat Pudina Chutney
(Walnut and Mint Chutney)

a small bunch of fresh mint leaves or 2 tablespoons dried mint
$1/2$ teaspoon chilli powder
500ml (16 fl oz) yogurt, beaten
6-8 walnuts, shelled
salt to taste

Preparation time: 15-20 minutes

1. Put the mint leaves, chilli powder, and a little of the yogurt, into a blender and process well.
2. Add the walnuts and blend until the walnuts have been coarsely ground.
3. Add the remaining yogurt and salt to taste and blend for a few seconds.

Unsuitable for freezing.

Murgh Kesari Pakora
(Saffron Chicken Snack)
SERVES 4-6

*C*hicken pieces are first cooked in milk with saffron and spices and then dipped in a rice batter for a mouth-watering snack. This dish looks as good as it tastes. I always soak the rice used for the batter, though to save time rice flour can be substituted. Rice flour is available from most Asian grocers.

1kg (2 lb) skinned, boneless chicken breasts
500ml (16 fl oz) milk
$^1/_2$ teaspoon saffron
4 whole cloves
2.5cm (1 inch) piece cinnamon stick
1 bay leaf
3 teaspoons aniseed or fennel seeds
8 green cardamom seeds
salt to taste

For the batter:
60g (2 oz) Basmati rice or 150g (5 oz) rice flour
1 teaspoon ground fennel
$1^1/_2$ teaspoons chilli powder
125ml (4 fl oz) natural yogurt
salt to taste
oil for frying

Preparation time: $1^1/_2$ hours
Cooking time: 30 minutes

1. Cut the chicken into 2.5cm (1 inch) cubes.
2. Put the chicken, milk, saffron, all the spices and salt to taste into a pan. Bring to the boil and then simmer on a low heat until the chicken is tender. Remove the chicken, strain the stock and keep to one side.
3. Soak the rice in cold water for 1 hour. Drain and grind in a blender with the fennel, chilli powder, and about 200ml (7 fl oz) of the reserved chicken stock, until the mixture has a thick consistency. Alternatively, mix the rice flour with the spices and water.
4. Whisk the yogurt and salt to taste into the rice paste and mix well.
5. Heat the oil in a deep frying pan, and then lower the heat to medium. Dip the chicken pieces into the batter and fry until golden brown and crisp. Drain on kitchen paper.

Serve hot with a chutney of your choice.

Unsuitable for freezing.

Murgh Kesari Pakora and Nadhru Kebab (p.20) with mango chutney.

Nadhru Kebab
(*Lotus Root Kebab*)
SERVES 4-6

*I*f using fresh lotus roots they should be thoroughly washed and boiled until tender *before use. I have used canned lotus root which is more readily available and can be bought from most Oriental grocers.*

500g (1 lb) canned lotus root, drained

2 medium potatoes

125ml (4 fl oz) lightly salted water

$^1/_2$ teaspoon ground ginger

2-3 tablespoons gram (chickpea) flour

1 teaspoon ground cummin

1 teaspoon garam masala

$^1/_2$ teaspoon chilli powder

2-3 green chillies, seeded and finely chopped (optional)

1 teaspoon pomegranate seeds, pounded, or a little lemon juice

2 tablespoons fresh coriander leaves, finely chopped

1 tablespoon fresh mint leaves, finely chopped (optional)

mustard oil for frying

Preparation time: 10 minutes
Cooking time: 45 minutes

1. Cut the lotus root into 1cm ($^1/_2$ inch) slices. Peel and cut the potatoes into small cubes.

2. Boil the potatoes and lotus root with the water in a pan, until the potatoes are cooked. Ensure that all the liquid has evaporated.

3. Remove the pan from the heat and mash the potato-lotus root mixture. Add the ground ginger, gram flour, ground cummin, garam masala, chilli powder, green chillies, pomegranate seeds or lemon juice, fresh coriander and mint leaves and mix to a dough.

4. Lightly oil your hands and shape small pieces of the dough into balls or flat patty shapes.

5. Heat the oil in a deep pan until almost smoking and then lower the heat to medium and fry the lotus root kebabs. At first, fry one kebab to make sure that it does not break up in the oil. If this does happen, then add some more gram flour to the lotus root mixture. Fry all the kebabs in this manner until crisp and brown.

Serve hot with the chutney of your choice.

Unsuitable for freezing.

Kashmiri Makki Akroat
(Corn and Walnut Snack)
SERVES 4-6

This quick snack is a great favourite in our household. When they are in season, fresh walnuts and almonds make this dish even more sumptuous.

625g (1¼ lb) fresh or frozen
  sweetcorn
125ml (4 fl oz) ghee or oil
salt to taste
125g (4 oz) almonds, blanched
  and slivered
60g (2 oz) walnuts, shelled
2-3 green chillies, seeded and
  minced
lime juice to taste
3-4 tablespoons fresh coriander
  leaves, finely chopped

Preparation time: 10 minutes
Cooking time: 30 minutes

1. Cook the sweetcorn until tender.
2. Heat the ghee or oil in a large pan, preferably non-stick. Add the sweetcorn and stir-fry for 1-2 minutes. Add the salt, nuts and green chillies.
3. Reduce the heat and stir the mixture until the nuts are golden brown.
4. Sprinkle the lime juice and fresh coriander over the top and serve immediately.

Serve with Kashmiri Dahi.

Unsuitable for freezing.

Kashmiri Dahi
SERVES 4-6

Kashmiris are unique in using saffron in a yogurt dish. The saffron lends colour and a subtle aroma to the yogurt for an enticing and luxurious raita.

3 tablespoons raisins
375ml (12 fl oz) natural yogurt
2 walnuts, shelled and finely
  chopped
1 tablespoon caster sugar
6 strands saffron, soaked in 2
  tablespoons hot water

Preparation time: 5 minutes

1. Wash the raisins and pat them dry.
2. Put the yogurt in a bowl and beat well.
3. Add all the ingredients to the yogurt and mix well. Chill before serving.

Serve as an accompaniment.

Unsuitable for freezing.

Murgh Reshmi Kebab
(Silken Chicken Kebabs)
SERVES 4

*R*eshmi Kebabs are normally cooked on open coal fires, but a normal grill is *adequate. These chicken kebabs are known for their silken texture. Cooked on the coal fires they have a smoky grilled taste on the outside whilst remaining tender and succulent on the inside.*

500-625g (1-1¼ lb) skinned, boneless chicken breasts
125ml (4 fl oz) oil
4 tablespoons distilled malt or white wine vinegar
4 cloves garlic, puréed
2.5cm (1 inch) piece fresh root ginger, puréed
1 teaspoon garam masala
½ teaspoon ground coriander
1 teaspoon ground cummin
½ teaspoon ground black pepper
3 tablespoons fresh coriander leaves, finely chopped
salt to taste
500ml (16 fl oz) natural yogurt
1 small onion, sliced and separated into rings
a little lemon juice

Preparation time: 10 minutes plus marinating
Cooking time: 15-20 minutes

1. Cut the chicken into 3.5cm (1½ inch) cubes.
2. Mix together the oil, vinegar, garlic, ginger, garam masala, coriander, cummin, black pepper, 2 tablespoons of fresh coriander, salt to taste and the yogurt. Put this marinade into a dish and stir in the chicken pieces. Cover and leave for at least 4 hours, or preferably overnight, in a refrigerator.
3. Thread the marinated chicken cubes onto metal or bamboo skewers, leaving a little space in between each piece of chicken.
4. Place under a hot grill and cook until golden brown. Baste the chicken occasionally with the remaining marinade.
5. To serve, sprinkle with the remaining fresh coriander and scatter over the onion rings. Sprinkle some lemon juice on top just before serving.

Serve hot with Naan bread.

Suitable for freezing.

Murgh Reshmi Kebab, Galavat Ke Kebab (p.24) with Akroat Pudina Chutney (p.17).

Galavat Ke Kebab
(Kashmiri Griddle Kebab)
SERVES 4

The best kebabs are said to melt in the mouth and these are very soft and should be handled with extreme care to avoid breaking.

500g (1 lb) lean lamb or beef mince
125ml (4 fl oz) water
6 black peppercorns
seeds from 2 brown cardamom pods
1 teaspoon ground coriander
4 whole cloves
90g (3 oz) channa dal, (split yellow chick-peas)
3 tablespoons raw papaya, (optional)
2 medium onions, grated
$^{1}/_{2}$ teaspoon paprika
$^{1}/_{2}$ teaspoon chilli powder
salt to taste
4-5 tablespoons oil

Preparation time: 30 minutes plus 2-3 hours resting time.
Cooking time: 45 minutes

1. Cook the mince with the water until the meat is tender and the liquid has evaporated. Put in a food processor and blend for 1 minute.
2. Dry roast the peppercorns, cardamom seeds, coriander, cloves, and channa dal separately until lightly browned and then grind them together in a coffee mill.
3. Grind together the papaya (if used), grated onion, paprika and chilli powder.
4. Add the spice mixture, the papaya mixture, and salt to taste to the puréed meat and knead the mixture well. Cover and put to one side in a cool place for 2-3 hours for the flavours to blend.
5. Knead the mixture again and shape into 8-10 balls.
6. Heat a griddle or non-stick frying pan. Brush the pan with a little oil and press the kebab balls onto the griddle with your fingers. Fry on both sides until well browned, adding a little oil each time a kebab is fried.

Serve with Akroat Pudina Chutney (p.17).

Unsuitable for freezing.

Kashmiri Pasande
(Kashmiri Lamb Fillet)
SERVES 4-6

*F*or this dish it is important that lean lamb fillets are used. The gravy from this dish *can be reduced and the fillets can be served as a starter or light snack with Akroat Pudina Chutney (see p.17).*

1kg (2 lb) lean lamb fillets
500ml (16 fl oz) natural yogurt
salt to taste
5cm (2 inch) piece fresh root
  ginger, ground to a paste
5cm (2 inch) cinnamon stick
3 brown cardamom pods
3-4 bay leaves
2 teaspoons aniseed
250ml (8 fl oz) ghee
$^{1}/_{4}$ teaspoon asafoetida, mixed
  with 250ml (8 fl oz) water
1 teaspoon cummin seeds
2 teaspoons ground coriander
1-2 teaspoons garam masala
250ml (8 fl oz) water

Preparation time: 30 minutes
Cooking time: 45-60 minutes

1. Cut the meat into strips 1 x 5 x 10cm ($^{1}/_{2}$ x 2 x 4 inch). Beat each strip with a mallet on one side to flatten them. These are called pasandas.
2. Mix together the yogurt, salt, ginger, cinnamon, cardamoms, bay leaves and aniseed.
3. Place the beaten pasandas in this mixture and stir well.
4. Heat the ghee in a large frying pan and add the pasandas and yogurt. Lower the heat, partially cover and leave to simmer on low until all the liquid has evaporated.
5. Remove the cover and stir-fry the meat gradually adding the asafoetida water. Stir continuously until the meat begins to brown.
6. Add the cummin, coriander and garam masala and continue stir-frying.
7. Add the water and simmer until the meat is tender. The pasandas are ready to serve when there is only very little gravy remaining. Remove any extra oil before serving and discard any whole spices as they are not to be eaten.

Serve with Kashmiri Naan.

Suitable for freezing.

LAMB DISHES

Kamargah
(Kashmiri Lamb Chops)
SERVES 4

*T*his is a very famous Kashmiri dish. It can be either served as a starter or as a main dish. The chops are firstly simmered in milk which imparts a sweet and pleasant flavour.

8 black peppercorns
1 teaspoon aniseed
5 green cardamom pods
1 small stick cinnamon
5 whole cloves
2 bay leaves
12 cutlets of lamb with 1 rib per cutlet
500ml (16 fl oz) milk
375ml (12 fl oz) water
4 tablespoons gram (chick-pea) flour
4 tablespoons rice flour
125ml (4 fl oz) water for the batter
1/2-1 teaspoon chilli powder
a pinch of asafoetida
salt to taste
125ml (4 fl oz) ghee or oil

Preparation time: 10 minutes
Cooking time: 50 minutes

1. Put the peppercorns, aniseed, cardamoms, cinnamon, cloves and bay leaves onto a square of muslin and tie the cloth together.
2. Put the meat, milk, water and spice bag into a large wide pan. Bring to the boil and cook uncovered for 25 minutes until the meat is tender and the liquid has almost evaporated.
3. Mix the gram flour, rice flour and water together and make into a thin batter. Beat the batter to a light consistency. To test the batter, drop a teaspoon of it into a cup of water. If the batter floats the consistency is correct - if not beat again.
4. Add the chilli, asafoetida, and salt to the batter and beat well.
5. Heat the ghee in a frying pan. Dip the pieces of meat in the batter and fry until golden brown.

Serve hot with Kashmiri Dahi (p.21) and Sheermal (p.90) or any other Naan.

Suitable for freezing.

Previous pages: Rogan Josh (p.29), Kamargah with aubergine pickle.

Rogan Josh
(Lamb Curry)
SERVES 4-6

*T*here are many variations of Rogan Josh and so many interpretations of the words. *Most cooks perceive their Rogan Josh recipe as being the epitome. The charm of Kashmiri cooking is the non-existence of thickening agents. Kashmiri Rogan Josh differs from the North Indian version as Kashmiris do not use onion and garlic. It is the addition of asafoetida that gives the dish its unique flavour.*

3-4 tablespoons ghee or oil
1 pinch asafoetida
1kg (2 lb) lamb or mutton, cut
   into 2.5cm(1 inch cubes)
4 whole cloves
1-2 teaspoons salt or to taste
125ml (4 fl oz) natural yogurt,
   mixed with 125ml (4 fl oz)
   water and well beaten
2$\frac{1}{2}$ teaspoons Kashmiri red
   chilli powder or $\frac{1}{2}$ - 1 teaspoon chilli powder with 2
   teaspoons paprika
1 tablespoon ground roasted
   coriander seeds
$\frac{1}{2}$ teaspoon ground ginger
1-2 tablespoons clotted or
   double cream, beaten
a pinch of saffron, soaked in 1
   tablespoon hot milk
4 green cardamom pods,
   crushed
a pinch of ground nutmeg
500-750ml (16-18 fl oz) hot
   water
1 teaspoon garam masala

Preparation time: 30 minutes
Cooking time: 45-60 minutes

1. Put the ghee in a large pan on a medium heat. Add the asafoetida, lamb, cloves and salt. Cover and simmer until the liquid has evaporated.

2. Pour a few tablespoons of the yogurt-water mixture around the meat and stir on medium to low heat.

3. Add the chilli powder and keep adding the yogurt-water mixture, stirring continuously. This is called the Bhunau method.

4. Add the ground coriander and ginger and 'Bhunau' again until all the yogurt-water has been used up and the meat is well browned.

5. Blend in the beaten clotted cream, saffron-milk, cardamoms and nutmeg. Stir and then add hot water to just cover the meat. Boil for a minute and then lower the heat.

6. Simmer until the meat is tender and the gravy coats the meat and the oil floats to the top. To serve, sprinkle the garam masala over the top.

Serve hot with Kashmiri Roti or Naan.

Suitable for freezing.

Zardhalo Boti
(Apricot and Meat Casserole)
SERVES 4

*K*ashmir is noted for the quality of its fresh fruit and vegetables. These are dried and stored for the severe winter months. In this form they give a slight sweet and sour taste to any dish. The dried apricots, jaggery and vinegar gives extra zest to this recipe.

125g (4 oz) whole dried apricots, stones removed
250ml (8 fl oz) water
3 tablespoons ghee or oil
3 medium onions, finely chopped
2.5cm (1 inch piece) fresh root ginger, peeled and ground to a paste
4-6 cloves garlic, peeled and ground to a paste
1 teaspoon chilli powder
1 teaspoon ground cummin
500g (1 lb) boneless lamb or mutton, cubed
500ml (16 fl oz) hot water
salt to taste
2-3 tablespoons white wine vinegar or lemon juice
15g (¹/₂ oz) jaggery
1 teaspoon garam masala
2 tablespoons fresh coriander leaves, finely chopped
1 tablespoon almonds, blanched and slivered

Preparation time: 1 hour 15 minutes
Cooking time: 1 hour

1. Soak the apricots in the water for 1 hour.
2. Heat the oil in a heavy-based pan and fry the onions until light brown.
3. Add the ginger and garlic pastes, chilli powder, and ground cummin and fry well.
4. Add the lamb and stir-fry, adding 250ml (8 fl oz) hot water, a little at a time, until the meat is well browned.
5. Add the remaining 250ml (8 fl oz) hot water and simmer on a low heat until the meat is tender.
6. Add the drained apricots and cook for at least 15 minutes, on a low heat.
7. Add the salt to taste, vinegar, jaggery and the garam masala. Stir well and cook for a further 10 minutes. Serve garnished with the fresh coriander and slivered almonds.

Serve hot with Naan bread.

Suitable for freezing.

Zardhalo Boti with Naan.

Marzwangan Korma
(Kashmiri Lamb Korma)
SERVES 4-6

*T*his is a speciality of renowned Kashmiri cooks known as wazas. It is normally made with Kashmiri red chillies which have a unique red colour and taste - a good red paprika is substituted in this recipe.

30g (1 oz) ball or 2 tablespoons
   tamarind
250ml (8 fl oz) boiling water
1kg (2 lb) boneless shoulder of
   lamb, cut into cubes
$^1/_2$ teaspoon ground turmeric
salt to taste
500ml (16 fl oz) water
4 tablespoons ghee or oil
4 green cardamom pods,
   crushed
2.5cm (1 inch) cinnamon stick
6-8 whole cloves
$^3/_4$ teaspoon ground aniseed
$^3/_4$ teaspoon chilli powder
2 tablespoons bright red
   paprika
$^1/_2$ teaspoon ground ginger

Preparation time: 1 hour 20 minutes
Cooking time: 45-60 minutes

1. Soak the tamarind in the boiling water and leave to soak for 1 hour. Press the tamarind through a strainer by rubbing and releasing as much pulp as possible.
2. Put the lamb, turmeric, salt and water into a pan and bring to the boil. Lower the heat and leave to simmer until the meat is tender. Strain the meat and retain the stock (yakhni).
3. Heat the ghee or oil in a heavy-based pan and add the crushed cardamoms, cinnamon, cloves, aniseed, chilli powder, paprika, ginger, tamarind pulp and salt to taste. Stir continuously on a medium to low heat until the oil floats to the top.
4. Add the meat and mix for 2-3 minutes. Add the reserved stock. Lower the heat, cover and simmer for 5-10 minutes. If the gravy is excessive increase the heat and reduce the liquid by boiling. There should be a small amount of gravy and the oil should float to the top.

Serve hot with rice.

Suitable for freezing.

Rishta
(Kashmiri Koftas)
SERVES 4-6

*T*his is a delicious dish as the koftas are so soft they literally melt in your mouth. These koftas are shaped like sausages and no binding agents are used in preparation, thus giving the koftas a more distinctive taste. The finer the meat is ground the more delectable this Kashmiri dish and the more celebrated is the chef.

30g (1 oz) fresh root ginger, ground to a paste

2 green chillies, ground to a paste

a tiny pinch asafoetida, mixed with 1 tablespoon water

6-8 brown cardamoms, crushed

4 teaspoons ground coriander

1 teaspoon black cummin seeds

1 teaspoon chilli powder

1/2 teaspoon garam masala

2 tablespoons Greek yogurt

500g (1 lb) finely minced fresh lamb

90g (3 oz) ghee or oil

1 teaspoon salt to taste

4-5 tablespoons hot water

1 tablespoon fresh chopped coriander leaves

Preparation time: 30 minutes
Cooking time: 25-30 minutes

1. Mix the ginger and chilli pastes with the asafoetida liquid, brown cardamoms, 2 teaspoons ground coriander, black cummin seeds, 1/2 teaspoon chilli powder, and the garam masala.

2. Mix the spice mixture with the yogurt to make a paste. Add this to the lamb mince along with 30g (1 oz) ghee and salt to taste. Knead the mixture until it is pliable. Divide into 16-18 pieces.

3. Roll each piece into a sausage shape about 5-6cm (2 - 2½ inch) in length. Press the sausages firmly into shape otherwise they are liable to break while cooking.

4. Add the remaining ghee to a non-stick frying pan. Place the koftas in a single layer in the pan. Cover and cook over a medium heat, shaking gently every now and then, taking care not to break the sausages.

5. Once they are a deep brown colour, add remaining 1/2 teaspoon chilli powder and lower the heat. Cook for a few minutes.

6. Add the remaining ground coriander and 4-5 tablespoons hot water, a little at a time. Simmer until the koftas are tender and all the moisture has evaporated and only the ghee remains. Sprinkle with the fresh coriander and serve.

Serve hot with any Kashmiri Naan or Roti.

Suitable for freezing.

Shalgum Gosht
(Turnip Meat Curry)
SERVES 4

*K*ashmiri turnips are seasonal but extremely versatile. They may be pickled, cooked on their own, served as an addition to meat, or even eaten raw.

500g (1 lb) small young turnips
salt
125ml (4 fl oz) natural yogurt
 mixed with 250ml (8 fl oz)
 water
125ml (4 fl oz) natural yogurt
^{1}/$_2$ teaspoon ground cloves
1 teaspoon ground cardamom
2.5cm (1 inch) piece fresh root
 ginger, peeled and ground to
 a paste
4-6 cloves garlic, peeled and
 ground to a paste
4-5 tablespoons ghee or oil
4 medium onions, finely sliced
1kg (2 lb) lamb or mutton, cut
 into 2.5cm (1 inch) cubes
1 teaspoon chilli powder
1 teaspoon paprika
500ml (16 fl oz) water
1 teaspoon garam masala
1-2 tablespoons fresh coriander
 leaves, finely chopped

Preparation time: 20 minutes
Cooking time: 1 hour 30 minutes

1. Peel the turnips, prick them with a fork, rub them with salt and leave for 30 minutes.
2. Squeeze out the excess water from the turnips and then boil them in the yogurt-water mixture until they are almost tender.
3. Remove the turnips from the yogurt-water and press out any extra moisture. Mix all this liquid with 125ml (4 fl oz) yogurt, ^{1}/$_4$ teaspoon ground cloves, ^{1}/$_2$ teaspoon ground cardamom, and ^{1}/$_2$ the quantity of the ginger and garlic pastes. Set aside.
4. In a heavy-based pan heat the ghee or oil and add the onions. Fry until light brown. Add the meat and fry, adding the remaining spices, chilli powder, paprika and salt to taste. Continue cooking and stirring until the oil comes to the surface and all the liquid has evaporated.
5. Gradually, add the spiced yogurt a little at time and stir-fry the meat until all the yogurt has been absorbed.
6. Add 500ml (16 fl oz) water to the meat. Cover and leave on low to simmer until the meat is tender.
7. Add the turnips and the garam masala and continue stirring on a low heat until the meat and the turnips are cooked and the ghee or oil floats to the top. Sprinkle with the fresh coriander and serve.

Serve hot with rice or chapattis.

Suitable for freezing.

Shalgum Gosht, Kalia Kesar (p.36) with Indian bread.

Kalia Kesar
(Saffron Meat)
SERVES 4-6

This recipe was created for the Mogul kings on their visits to Kashmir as a delicacy for the winter months. Much of Kashmiri cuisine has a Moghlai flavour due to the large influence of the Mogul Kings on Kashmir. Indeed it was the Moguls who described Kashmir as the Land of Paradise.

125ml (4 fl oz) ghee, oil or butter
2 small onions, thinly sliced
1kg (2 lb) boneless lamb or mutton, cut into 5cm (2 inch) cubes
1 tablespoon ground coriander
8-10 cloves garlic, ground to a paste
3 tablespoons almonds, blanched and ground
180ml (6 fl oz) natural yogurt
600ml (1 pint) hot water
1/2-1 teaspoon saffron, soaked and dissolved in 1 tablespoon hot water
1/2-1 teaspoon garam masala
salt to taste
1 tablespoon kewda water (optional)
125ml (4 fl oz) single cream

Preparation time: 30 minutes
Cooking time: 1 hour 20 minutes

1. Heat the ghee in a heavy-based pan and fry the sliced onions until golden brown. Remove them from the oil and process in a blender. Set aside.
2. In the same pan, add the meat and stir-fry for 1-2 minutes. Add the ground coriander, garlic paste, ground almonds and 'bhunau' (stir-fry on a low heat) by gradually mixing in the yogurt a little at a time.
3. Add the hot water and simmer on a low heat until the meat is tender and only about 300ml (1/2 pint) of water remains. Remove the pan from the heat.
4. Remove the meat from the stock ensuring that the spices remain behind. Strain the liquid from the pan through muslin.
5. Replace the pan on the heat with the strained stock. Add the meat, the fried ground onions, saffron water, garam masala and the salt to taste.
6. Cover the pan lightly and simmer on a very low heat for 5-10 minutes until the oil comes to the surface. Remove any excess oil and add the kewda water, if used, and cream just before serving.

Serve with any Kashmiri bread.

Suitable for freezing.

Gushtaba
(Meatball Curry)
SERVES 4-6

*W*azas *(speciality Kashmiri cooks) often use this recipe at weddings or other celebratory banquets. It is a rich and creamy dish said to be the Cashmere of all Kashmiri dishes. This is a Muslim recipe cooked with onions; the Hindu Brahmin Kashmiris cook without onions and garlic, using asafoetida instead.*

1kg (2 lb) lamb mince
2.5 cm (1 inch) piece fresh root ginger, peeled and ground to a paste
3 cloves garlic, peeled and ground to a paste
1/2 teaspoon grated nutmeg
4 brown cardamoms, crushed
1 tablespoon ghee
125g (4 oz) almonds, blanched and toasted
250ml (8 fl oz) single cream
500ml (16 fl oz) milk
500ml (16 fl oz) natural yogurt
125g (4 oz) ghee or oil
2 large onions, minced
1 tablespoon ground coriander
1 tablespoon ground cummin
1 teaspoon garam masala
1 teaspoon chilli powder
salt to taste
1/4 teaspoon saffron, soaked in 1 tablespoon hot water
2 tablespoons fresh coriander leaves, chopped

Preparation time: 30 minutes
Cooking time: 45 minutes

1. Mix the lamb with the ginger, garlic, nutmeg, and cardamoms. Beat with a wooden meat mallet, adding a little ghee now and then, until the mince mixture becomes very smooth. The art of making a perfect Gushtaba lies in attaining the correct consistency of the minced meat. Form the mixture into 2.5cm (1 inch) balls and set aside.
2. Finely slice or sliver the almonds.
3. Mix together the cream, milk and yogurt and strain through a muslin cloth.
4. Heat the ghee or oil in a heavy-based pan and sauté the onions until all the moisture evaporates and the onions become translucent.
5. Add the coriander, cummin, garam masala, chilli powder, cream mixture and salt to taste. Mix well. Bring to the boil, then gently lower the meatballs into the sauce.
6. Cover and cook on a low heat, gently shaking the pan from time to time, taking care not to break the meatballs. Allow the meatballs to cook through and become firm.
7. Before serving, sprinkle with the saffron water, fresh coriander and the slivered almonds.

Serve hot with Kashmiri Roti or rice.

Unsuitable for freezing.

Kashmiri Raan
(Seasoned Leg of Lamb)
SERVES 8-10

*K*ashmir is renowned for its excellent lamb. In this recipe the leg of lamb is marinated in yogurt, spices, nuts and honey and then baked. The leftover meat can be eaten cold or added to vegetables.

2.3kgs (5 lb) leg of lamb
2 tablespoons finely grated
 fresh root ginger
6 cloves garlic, crushed
1 teaspoon ground cummin
1 teaspoon ground turmeric
1 teaspoon freshly ground
 black pepper
$^1/_2$ teaspoon ground cinnamon
1 teaspoon ground cardamom
$^1/_2$ teaspoon ground cloves
2-3 tablespoons lemon juice
2 tablespoons ghee or oil
250ml (8 fl oz) natural yogurt
2 tablespoons almonds,
 blanched
2 tablespoons shelled pistachio
 nuts
$^1/_2$ teaspoon saffron, soaked in
 2 tablespoons hot water
1 tablespoon clear honey
1-2 teaspoons salt or to taste

Preparation time: 15 minutes plus marinating
Cooking time: as per weight

1. Remove any skin and excess fat from the lamb. Using the point of a sharp knife, cut deep gashes into the lamb.
2. Mix together the ginger, garlic, all the ground spices, lemon juice and the ghee or oil. Rub the spice mixture all over the lamb, making sure to push it into the slashed pockets.
3. Put the yogurt, almonds, pistachios, saffron and liquid into a blender and process until smooth. Spread the yogurt mixture over the lamb.
4. Drizzle over the honey and cover the lamb. Allow to marinate at least overnight in the refrigerator or if possible for 2 days.
5. Preheat the oven to 230°C, 450°F, Gas Mark 8. The meat should cook for approximately 30 minutes per pound of meat. Roast the lamb in a covered baking dish for 30 minutes, then reduce the heat to moderate 190°C, 375°F, Gas Mark 5 and cook for a further $1^3/_4$ hours or until the lamb is cooked through. Uncover the lamb and allow to cool to room temperature before serving.

Serve with any pulao.

Suitable for freezing.

Kashmiri Raan and Yakhni Pulao (p.100).

Kashmiri Aab Gosht
(Milky Meat)
SERVES 4

*L*amb cooked with milk tastes similar to veal and makes a tender and mouth-watering meal. Aab Gosht is a very famous Kashmiri dish, expertly prepared by the wazas (Kashmiri chefs) and served sumptuously on festive occasions. No festivity is complete without the famous Kashmiri Aab Gosht.

500g (1 lb) lamb, cut into
   7.5cm (3 inch) pieces
Approx. 750ml (24 fl oz) water
4 green cardamom pods, lightly
   crushed
2 cloves garlic, lightly crushed
7.5cm (3 inch) cinnamon stick
1 teaspoon salt
8 black peppercorns

For the milk broth:
1 litre (32 fl oz) full cream milk
8 green cardamom pods, lightly
   crushed
10cm (4 inch) cinnamon stick
1 teaspoon salt

$1/4$ teaspoon ground ginger
125ml (4 fl oz) whipping cream
125g (4 oz) whole almonds,
   blanched

Preparation time: 30 minutes
Cooking time: 1 hour 30 minutes

1. Place the meat in a heavy medium-sized saucepan and cover with the water. Bring to the boil and skim off any scum that rises to the surface.
2. Add the cardamoms, garlic, cinnamon, salt and peppercorns and simmer, uncovered, until the meat is tender. The water should have reduced to 300ml ($1/2$ pint) - if it has not, then remove the meat and reduce the water by boiling rapidly. Strain the stock and set aside.
3. Meanwhile, in a separate pan, make the milk broth. Boil the milk with the cardamoms, cinnamon and salt, stirring continuously, over a medium to high heat until it reduces to 500ml (16 fl oz).
4. Slowly, mix the meat broth with the milk broth. Add the meat and the ground ginger and cook for 10 minutes or until most of the liquid has evaporated.
5. Purée the whipping cream and almonds together in a blender. Just before serving, add this purée to the meat. Heat through gently and serve.

Serve hot with rice.

Unsuitable for freezing.

Yakhni Kofta Curry
(Meatballs in Stock)
SERVES 4

*M*any Kashmiri recipes are age-old and are passed secretively from mother to daughter, it is thus with much coaxing that a friend finally shared the secrets of this dish with me.

For the Koftas:
500g (1 lb) lamb mince
1 green chilli
1 tablespoon ground coriander
1 egg
1 tablespoon semolina
$^1/_2$ teaspoon ground aniseed
1 teaspoon garlic purée
salt to taste
1 tablespoon ghee or oil

For the Yakhni Meat Stock:
1kg (2 lb) lamb bones
1 litre ($1^3/_4$ pints) milk
a few whole black peppercorns

1-2 tablespoons ghee or oil
1 teaspoon black cummin seeds
1 teaspoon ground black
 pepper
350ml (12 fl oz) natural yogurt,
 beaten
salt to taste

Preparation time: 1-2 hours
Cooking time: 45 minutes

1. Put all the ingredients for the koftas into a food processor and grind to a fine paste. Set aside in the refrigerator.
2. In a heavy-based pan add all the ingredients for the yakhni meat stock and boil, covered, on a low heat for 1-2 hours adding 125ml (4 fl oz) water if required.
3. Strain the stock, discarding the bones.
4. Take the kofta mixture out of the refrigerator and shape into about 20 balls.
5. In a heavy-based pan heat the ghee, the cummin seeds and black pepper. Stir and add the koftas in a single layer. Fry on a high heat, shaking the pan from time to time, taking care not to break the koftas. Cook until they are firm.
6. Add the yakhni stock and simmer, uncovered, on a medium heat. Cook until the liquid is reduced by half. Remove from the heat and allow to cool slightly.
7. Add the beaten yogurt to the meatballs. Add the salt to taste and return the pan to the heat and simmer for 10 minutes, making sure it does not boil as this will curdle the yogurt.

Serve with boiled rice or bread.

Suitable for freezing.

Gosht Akbari

SERVES 4-6

*T**his exotic dish, accompanied by Saffron Rice, was served for Emperor Akbar on one of his many summer visits to Kashmir the Land of Bliss and Beauty. The dried prunes from India are slightly more sour than their English counterparts, so I have used tamarind to add a little sharpness to the dish.*

a marble-sized ball of tamarind
125g (4 oz) stoneless dates,
  chopped
125ml (4 fl oz) ghee or oil
1kg (2 lb) boneless lamb, cut
  into 2.5cm (1 inch) cubes
3 medium onions, chopped
500ml (16 fl oz) water
1-2 level teaspoons salt
2.5cm (1 inch) cinnamon stick
grated rind of $^1/_2$ a lemon
125g (4 oz) fresh apricots,
  stoned and washed
125g (4 oz) dried stoned prunes
125g (4 oz) raisins
2 tablespoons brown sugar
1 teaspoon garam masala
$^1/_2$ teaspoon chilli powder
6-8 green chillies, slit
  lengthwise

Preparation time: 30 minutes
Cooking time: Approx. 1 hour

1. Soak the tamarind in hot water for about 30 minutes. Squeeze out all the pulp by pressing through a sieve.
2. Cook the chopped dates in a pan with a little water until the dates soften. Press through a sieve to purée.
3. Heat half of the ghee in a heavy-based pan and fry the lamb until brown. Remove the meat from the ghee and set aside.
4. Add the remaining ghee to the pan, and cook the onions until golden brown. Reduce the heat and add 250ml (8 fl oz) water, salt, cinnamon, lemon rind and fried meat. Simmer uncovered for 20 minutes and then add another 250ml (8 fl oz) water. Cover and cook for a further 20 minutes.
5. Add the date purée, apricots, prunes, raisins, brown sugar, garam masala, chilli powder and tamarind pulp. Stir well and add more water if necessary. Cover and simmer gently for 20-30 minutes until the meat is tender and very little gravy remains. Serve garnished with the green chillies.

Serve hot with Saffron Rice.

Suitable for freezing.

Gosht Akbari and Kesar Mattar Pulao (p.101).

Tabak Maaz
(Rib Lamb Chops)
SERVES 4-6

*T*abak Maaz is often served at Wazawaans, the festive banquets celebrating weddings and births. No Wazawaan is complete without this dish and it is often the pride of the wazas (Kashmiri chefs). It is a truly regal dish and must be tried!

12 rib lamb chops
500ml (16 fl oz) full cream
  milk
1 teaspoon ground ginger
1 teaspoon ground aniseed
2-3 whole cloves
2 bay leaves
salt to taste
4-5 tablespoons ghee or oil
1 teaspoon garam masala
1 teaspoon chilli powder
1 teaspoon mango powder
  (amchoor)
silver leaf for garnishing
  (optional)

Preparation time: 30 minutes
Cooking time: 1 hour

1. Put the lamb chops, milk, ginger, aniseed, cloves, bay leaves and salt to taste into a heavy-based pan. Bring to the boil and then simmer on low until the lamb chops are tender and all the liquid has evaporated.
2. Heat the ghee in a non-stick frying pan and shallow fry the lamb chops until they are crisp.
3. Sprinkle on the garam masala, chilli powder and mango powder. Garnish with silver leaves if liked.

Serve hot with Kashmiri bread.

Suitable for freezing.

Dahiwala Keema
(Minced Meat with Yogurt)
SERVES 4

*A*nother speciality of the Kashmiri Brahmin who are past masters in handling both meat and sweetmeat. As well as a main course, this dish can be used as a filling for samosas, canapés or even as a topping.

5 tablespoons ghee or oil
2.5cm (1 inch) piece fresh root ginger, peeled and ground to a paste
3 cloves garlic, peeled and ground to a paste
500g (1 lb) coarsely minced lamb
1 teaspoon ground coriander
1 teaspoon ground cummin
$^1/_2$ teaspoon chilli powder
salt to taste
1 teaspoon sugar
500ml (16 fl oz) natural yogurt, beaten
2 tablespoons grated beetroot
$^1/_2$ teaspoon garam masala
1 tablespoon kewda water (optional)

Preparation time: 10 minutes
Cooking time: 45 minutes

1. Heat the ghee or oil in a heavy-based pan and add the ginger and garlic pastes and stir-fry for 1 minute.
2. Add the lamb, coriander, cummin, chilli powder, salt and sugar. Stir continuously until all the water has evaporated and the oil comes to the surface.
3. Add the yogurt, and beetroot. Mix well and leave to simmer on low for 20 minutes, stirring continuously.
4. The yogurt should begin to curdle and then resemble the minced meat. Stir-fry until all the liquid has evaporated.
5. Sprinkle with garam masala and the kewda water, if used, and serve.

Serve hot with Naan bread or Sheermal (p.90).

Suitable for freezing.

CHICKEN AND FISH

Murgh Khubani
(Apricot Chicken)
SERVES 4-6

A classic chicken dish of Kashmir cooked with dried apricots and aromatic spices.
Kashmir is noted for its apricot orchards. In this recipe chicken is cooked with
dried apricots to make a fruity and flavoursome dish. The kewda water, available
from most Asian grocers, gives the dish an aromatic fragrance.

1kg (2 - 2¼ lb) chicken
12 whole dried apricots, soaked
  for 1 hour in cold water
3 tablespoons ghee or oil
3 medium onions, finely sliced
5-6 cloves garlic, peeled and
  ground to a paste
2 tablespoons fresh root ginger,
  peeled and ground or finely
  chopped
3 green chillies, sliced
3 green cardamom pods,
  crushed
2.5cm (1 inch) cinnamon stick
3 medium tomatoes, chopped
1-2 teaspoons salt or to taste
500ml (16 fl oz) water
½ teaspoon saffron strands,
  soaked in 2 tablespoons hot
  milk or water
½ teaspoon Kashmiri garam
  masala (see page 9)
2 teaspoons kewda water
  (optional)

Preparation time: 1 hour 30 minutes
Cooking time: 50 minutes

1. Cut the chicken into 8 pieces and remove the
skin.
2. Drain the apricots and remove the stones if
necessary.
3. Heat the ghee or oil in a pan and fry the onions,
garlic, ginger, chillies, cardamoms and cinnamon
until the onions are golden brown in colour.
4. Add the chicken pieces, fry until golden and
then add the tomatoes and salt. Fry for a few
minutes until the oil separates out. Pour in the
water. Cover with a tight-fitting lid and reduce the
heat. Simmer over a low heat for 25 minutes.
5. Add the apricots and saffron to the pan. Stir
well. Cover again. Cook for a further 10 minutes
on a low heat, stirring carefully from time to time.
The apricots should not become mushy.
6. Stir in the garam masala. Remove from the
heat and sprinkle with kewda water if used.

Serve hot with rice or Kashmiri Roti (p.88).

Suitable for freezing.

Previous pages: Murgh Khubani and Murgh Dum (p.49).

Murgh Dum
SERVES 4-6

*D*um is a cooking technique frequently used in Northern India. The meat is allowed to cook in its own juices by sealing the pot with dough. Kashmiris use this Dum technique to achieve full flavours. In this recipe the combination of khoya (see page 10) and yogurt makes this dish a culinary masterpiece.

1kg (2-2^1/$_4$ lb) chicken
4 tablespoons khoya (see page 10), mixed with 4 table-spoons natural yogurt
20 almonds, blanched and crushed
^{1}/$_4$ teaspoon saffron, soaked in 1 tablespoon warm milk
^{1}/$_2$ teaspoon ground cardamom
4-5 tablespoons ghee or oil
a pinch asafoetida
^{1}/$_2$ teaspoon ground ginger
2.5cm (1 inch) piece fresh root ginger, peeled and ground to a paste
2.5cm (1 inch) cinnamon stick
^{1}/$_2$ -1 teaspoon chilli powder
salt to taste
250ml (8 fl oz) natural yogurt
500ml (16 fl oz) hot water
2-3 tablespoons fresh coriander leaves
^{1}/$_2$ teaspoon garam masala

Preparation time: 1 hour 30 minutes
Cooking time: 50 minutes

1. Cut the chicken into 8-10 pieces and remove the skin.
2. Combine the khoya mixture with the almonds, saffron and cardamom.
3. Heat the ghee or oil in a heavy-based pan, and add the asafoetida and chicken. Stir-fry and add the ground ginger, ginger paste, cinnamon, chilli powder and salt to taste. Add a little yogurt at a time, cooking well between each addition, until the chicken becomes golden brown. Stir in the water and cover tightly. Simmer on a low heat until the chicken is just cooked.
4. Add the khoya mixture and cover tightly. Cook on a low heat, stirring occasionally, until the chicken is cooked through and browned. The liquid should all evaporate and the oil float to the surface.
5. Sprinkle with the fresh coriander, garam masala and serve.

Serve with Chapattis or a rice pulao.

Suitable for freezing.

Sukha Adrakwala Murgh
(Ginger Chicken)
SERVES 4

*T*his dish has a sweet and sour flavour. Kashmiri red chillies are normally used in this dish, imparting a brilliant red colour, but I have substituted chilli powder and paprika.

2 medium onions, sliced
ghee or oil for frying
5cm (2 inch) piece fresh root
  ginger, peeled
6 cloves garlic, peeled
1 teaspoon ground coriander
1 teaspoon ground cummin
1 teaspoon chilli powder
$^1/_2$ teaspoon paprika
3 green cardamom pods,
  crushed
salt to taste
60ml (2 fl oz) malt vinegar
250ml (8 fl oz) natural yogurt
1 kg (2-2$^1/_4$ lb) chicken,
  skinned and cut into 8 pieces
3-4 tablespoons ghee or oil
1 teaspoon cummin seeds
3 tomatoes, chopped
1 teaspoon sugar (optional)
125ml (4 fl oz) water
2 tablespoons coriander leaves,
  finely chopped

Preparation time: 30 minutes plus 3 hours marinating
Cooking time: 45 minutes

1. Fry the sliced onions in a little ghee or oil, until golden brown and crisp. Remove, drain and set aside.
2. Grind the ginger and garlic to make a paste. Mix together the ginger/garlic paste, coriander, cummin, chilli powder, paprika, cardamoms, salt and malt vinegar.
3. Add the ground spice mixture to the yogurt and spread over the chicken pieces. Leave to marinate in a cool place for 3 hours.
4. Remove the chicken pieces and reserve the marinade. Heat 3-4 tablespoons ghee or oil in a pan and add the cummin seeds and the chicken pieces. Cook for 1 minute, then add the tomatoes. Mix thoroughly until blended. Mix in the reserved marinade and the sugar (if used) and continue stirring until the moisture has evaporated.
5. Add the water and leave to simmer on a low heat for 25 minutes or until the chicken is cooked.
6. Serve garnished with the fried onions and chopped coriander.

Serve with pulao rice.

Suitable for freezing.

Sukha Adrakwala Murgh.

Murgh Malai
(Spicy Cream Chicken)
SERVES 4-6

*I*n days gone by this dish was cooked on open coal fires. The marinated chicken pieces were placed in pots, sealed with dough and cooked on burning coals. This gave an intense flavour to the chicken. The combination of saffron and cream makes this a colourful and enticing dish.

2 medium onions, peeled and
  left whole
500ml (16 fl oz) natural yogurt
250ml (8 fl oz) single cream
180g (6 oz) butter, melted
salt to taste
1 teaspoon ground turmeric
1 teaspoon chilli powder
2 cloves garlic, minced
3 tablespoons almonds,
  blanched and ground
6 boneless chicken breasts,
  skinned
$^1/_2$ teaspoon saffron, soaked in 2
  tablespoons milk

Preparation time: 30 minutes plus 1 hour marinating
Cooking time: 1 hour

1. Boil the onions in water until soft. Drain and blend in a food processor along with the yogurt, cream, butter, salt, turmeric, chilli powder, garlic and almonds.
2. Grease a casserole dish and place the chicken breasts in the bottom in a single layer. Pour the paste over the chicken and mix well. Leave to marinate in a cool place for 1 hour.
3. Preheat the oven to 180°C, 350°F, Gas Mark 4. Cover the casserole with a tight-fitting lid or foil and bake in the oven for 30-40 minutes until the chicken is cooked. The butter will rise to the surface.
4. Just before serving, add the saffron to the dish and mix gently.

Serve hot with rice.

Unsuitable for freezing.

Palag Murgh
(Spinach Chicken)
SERVES 4-6

This dish can also be made with lamb or beef. Kashmiris are very fond of combining meat or fish with greens to create a colourful and appetising dish.

2-3 green chillies
500g (1 lb) fresh spinach,
   washed and dried
2 large onions
2.5cm (1 inch) piece fresh root
   ginger, peeled and ground to
   a paste
10-12 cloves garlic, peeled and
   ground to a paste
125ml (4 fl oz) ghee or oil
60ml (2 fl oz) milk
1kg (2-2$^1\!/_4$ lb) chicken, cut
   into 8 pieces and skinned
$^1\!/_2$ teaspoon chilli powder
1 teaspoon garam masala
salt to taste
3 tomatoes, finely chopped
125ml (4 fl oz) single cream

Preparation time: 45 minutes
Cooking time: 45 minutes

1. Put the green chillies and spinach into a blender or food processor and blend to a paste.
2. Separately, in a clean blender or food processor, grind the onions to a paste. Mix with the ginger and garlic pastes.
3. Heat the ghee or oil in a heavy-based pan. Add the onion, ginger and garlic pastes. Fry until pinkish-brown by adding a little milk to prevent the pastes from sticking to the bottom.
4. Add the chicken and fry for 1 minute. Add the chilli powder, garam masala, and salt to taste. Stir-fry until all the moisture evaporates and the oil separates out.
5. Mix in the spinach purée and tomatoes. Cover tightly and cook on a low heat for about 35 minutes or until the chicken is tender.
6. Remove the lid and if there is any liquid remaining then continue cooking and stirring until all the liquid evaporates and the oil separates out.
7. Just before serving, pour the cream over the chicken and serve immediately.

Serve hot with any Naan or bread.

Suitable for freezing without the cream.

Kesar Murgh
(Saffron Chicken)
SERVES 4-6

*K*ashmir is the only place in India where saffron, the world's most expensive spice, *is harvested. This simple dish glistens with a beautiful orange colour obtained from the aromatic saffron.*

1kg (2-2¼ lb) chicken
2.5cm (1 inch) piece fresh root ginger, peeled
3-4 cloves garlic, peeled
3 tablespoons butter or ghee
1 medium onion, finely chopped
2 green chillies, thinly sliced
½ teaspoon saffron, soaked in 2 tablespoons hot water
½ teaspoon ground cardamom
salt to taste
½ teaspoon freshly ground black pepper

Preparation time: 20 minutes
Cooking time: 30 minutes

1. Cut the chicken into 8-10 pieces and remove the skin.
2. Grind the ginger and garlic to a paste.
3. In a heavy-based pan melt the butter and add the onion, garlic-ginger paste and chillies and sauté until the onion becomes transparent.
4. Add the chicken pieces, stir and add the saffron water, ground cardamom and salt to taste. Mix thoroughly.
5. Cover and cook on a very low heat until the chicken is cooked and all the liquid has evaporated. This should take approximately 15-20 minutes.
6. Just before serving sprinkle the dish with freshly ground black pepper.

Serve hot with rice.

Suitable for freezing.

Badam Murgh (p.56) and Kesar Murgh with Kashmiri Roti (p.88).

Badam Murgh
(Almond Chicken)
SERVES 4-6

*S*pring in Kashmir is heralded with the appearance of almond blossoms. Much of Kashmiri cooking incorporates almonds and this dish is often called 100 Almond Chicken. Fresh mint is added to the dish for extra flavour and a fresh aroma.

100 almonds approx 125g
  (4 oz), blanched
500ml (16 fl oz) natural yogurt
5-6 tablespoons ghee or oil
1kg (2-2$^{1}/_{4}$ lb) chicken, cut into
  8 pieces and skinned
3 medium onions, finely sliced
6-8 cloves garlic, peeled and
  ground to a paste
2.5cm (1 inch) piece fresh root
  ginger, peeled and ground to
  a paste
8 small green cardamom pods
1 teaspoon chilli powder
$^{1}/_{2}$ teaspoon ground fennel
1 teaspoon black cummin
  seeds, ground
1 teaspoon ground coriander
$^{1}/_{2}$ teaspoon ground turmeric
4 medium tomatoes, chopped
1-2 teaspoons salt or to taste
4 tablespoons fresh mint leaves,
  chopped

Preparation time: 30 minutes
Cooking time: 45-60 minutes

1. Reserve 10 almonds. Grind the rest of the almonds with the yogurt in a blender or food processor and set aside. Slice the reserved 10 almonds and fry until golden brown and set aside.
2. Heat the ghee or oil in a heavy-based frying pan. Fry the chicken pieces until golden brown. Remove from the oil and set aside.
3. In the same pan, add the onions and fry on a low heat until golden. Do not allow to brown as this will change the colour of the sauce.
4. Add the garlic, ginger, cardamoms, chilli powder, fennel, ground black cummin seeds, coriander and turmeric and stir-fry for 2 minutes. Add the tomatoes, salt and 2 tablespoons of the mint. Cover and cook on a low heat, stirring frequently until the mixture thickens and the oil floats to the top.
5. Add the chicken pieces. Stir and add the almond-yogurt mixture. Cover and leave to simmer on a low heat until the chicken is cooked.
6. Serve garnished with the fried almonds and the remaining fresh mint.

Serve hot with rice or any Kashmiri bread.

Suitable for freezing.

Dhaniwala Murgh
(Coriander Chicken)
SERVES 4-6

*T*his is a colourful dish that can be made with chicken or meat. A speciality of the Wazas (Kashmiri chefs), it is served alongside Rogan Josh, Gushtaba, Gobi Dum, and Biryani at festive occasions.*

1 bunch coriander leaves, about
   15g (^{1}/$_2$ oz)
1kg (2-2^1/$_4$ lb) chicken, cut
   into 8 pieces and skinned
2 brown cardamom pods
^{1}/$_2$ teaspoon ground turmeric
500ml (16 fl oz) water
4-6 tablespoons ghee or oil
2 medium onions, finely sliced
3 whole cloves
4-5 green cardamom pods,
   crushed
2.5cm (1 inch) cinnamon stick
500-750ml (16-24 fl oz) natural
   yogurt, well beaten
6-7 cloves garlic, peeled and
   ground to a paste
salt to taste
^{1}/$_2$ teaspoon black pepper,
   freshly ground

Preparation time: 30 minutes
Cooking time: 40 minutes

1. Wash and clean the coriander by removing the leaves from their stalks and chop finely.
2. Put the chicken, brown cardamoms, turmeric, and water into a pan and cook on a low heat for 20 minutes or until the chicken is tender. Remove the chicken and strain the stock. Set aside.
3. Heat the ghee or oil in a heavy-based pan, and add the onions and fry until crisp and reddish brown in colour. Remove the onions and drain.
4. In the same oil, add the cloves, cardamom pods, cinnamon, yogurt and garlic and continue stirring on a medium heat until the sauce has thickened and the oil begins to separate out.
5. Add the boiled chicken and the salt to taste. Cook, stirring continuously until the sauce coats the chicken. Add the reserved stock. Cook, stirring from time to time, until the liquid reduces and just coats the chicken.
6. Just before serving, stir in the fried onions, ground black pepper and the fresh chopped coriander leaves.

Serve hot with rice or bread.

Suitable for freezing.

Murgh Noorjhani

SERVES 4

*T*his dish was specially made for Noorjahan, the consort of Jhangir (a renowned Moghul King). A splendid garden in Kashmir has also been named after her. A favourite with my family and friends this dish is very easy to make.

8 chicken drumsticks
6 tablespoons natural yogurt
4-6 cloves garlic, peeled and
   ground to a paste
2.5cm (1 inch) piece fresh root
   ginger, peeled and ground to
   a paste
4 tablespoons ghee or oil
2 medium onions, finely
   chopped
2 tomatoes, chopped
1 teaspoon ground cummin
2 teaspoons ground coriander
$\frac{1}{2}$ teaspoon chilli powder
$\frac{1}{2}$ teaspoon ground turmeric
2 tablespoons raisins
2 tablespoons unsalted cashew
   nuts, halved
salt to taste
500ml (16 fl oz) water
$\frac{1}{2}$ teaspoon garam masala
1 tablespoon fresh coriander
   leaves, finely chopped

Preparation time: 30 minutes plus 4 hours marinating
Cooking time: 30-40 minutes

1. Skin the chicken drumsticks and prick them all over with a fork.
2. Mix the yogurt with the garlic and ginger pastes and spread over the chicken. Leave in a cool place to marinate for 4 hours.
3. Heat the ghee or oil in a heavy-based saucepan and fry the onion until light brown. Add the tomatoes, cummin, coriander, chilli powder, turmeric, raisins, and cashew nuts. Continue stir-frying until all the moisture evaporates and the oil separates out.
4. Add the chicken and salt to taste. Cook over a low heat, stirring all the time. When the mixture begins to stick and the liquid has evaporated, add the water. Cover and leave to simmer on a low heat until the chicken is cooked.
5. Sprinkle on the garam masala and coriander leaves and serve.

Serve hot with Naan or Roti.

Suitable for freezing.

Murgh Noorjhani with Chapattis and tomato chutney.

Khatti Macchi
(Sour Fish)
SERVES 4-6

This particular dish can be served hot or cold. The sauce can be prepared earlier and when you are ready to eat, add the fish and water and cook accordingly. The tamarind gives the dish a tangy flavour which gives it its name.

1kg (2 lb) firm white fish, cut
   into steaks
salt for rubbing
oil for frying
2-3 tablespoons tamarind,
   soaked in 125ml (4 fl oz)
   boiling water for 1 hour
3 tablespoons oil
a pinch asafoetida
$^1/_2$ teaspoon cummin seeds
$^1/_2$ teaspoon ground turmeric
1 teaspoon ground ginger
1 teaspoon ground aniseed
1 teaspoon chilli powder
1 teaspoon garam masala
3 bay leaves
$^1/_2$ teaspoon ground cinnamon
1 teaspoon ground coriander
salt to taste
250ml (8 fl oz) water
$^1/_2$ -1 teaspoon sugar (optional)

Preparation time: 1 hour 20 minutes
Cooking time: 35 minutes

1. Wash and dry the fish and rub with a little salt.
2. Heat the oil in a deep pan and deep-fry the fish steaks until they are light brown in colour. Drain and put to one side.
3. Strain and sieve the soaked tamarind, making sure to extract all the pulp.
4. Heat the oil in a frying pan. Add the asafoetida, cummin seeds, turmeric and tamarind pulp. Mix well.
5. Add the remaining spices. Keep stirring until all the moisture evaporates and the oil comes to the surface. Add salt to taste.
6. Add the fish, water and sugar, if liked. Cover and cook until the fish is tender.

Serve hot or cold with rice.

Unsuitable for freezing.

Tariwale Macchi
(Spicy Fish)
SERVES 4

In this recipe the fish is cooked in a rich tomato and onion sauce and enhanced with yogurt and spices. Colourful and pleasant to the eye, this dish is a family favourite and is always a success.

4 fish steaks such as haddock,
  coley or cod
1 teaspoon salt for rubbing
1 tablespoon lime juice
4-5 tablespoons ghee or oil
3 medium onions, peeled and
  grated
6 cloves garlic, peeled and
  finely chopped
2.5cm (1 inch) piece fresh root
  ginger, peeled and grated
4 tomatoes, finely chopped
$1/2$ teaspoon salt to taste
$1/2$ teaspoon ground turmeric
1 teaspoon ground coriander
$1/2$ teaspoon chilli powder
$1/2$ teaspoon ground aniseed
$1/2$ teaspoon garam masala
125ml (4 fl oz) natural yogurt
1 tablespoon fresh mint leaves,
  finely chopped (optional)
1 tablespoon fresh coriander
  leaves, finely chopped

Preparation time: 30 minutes
Cooking time: 45 minutes

1. Wash and dry the fish. Rub the salt and lime juice over the fish and put to one side.
2. In a heavy frying pan, heat the oil or ghee and add the grated onions, garlic and ginger and fry until light brown.
3. Add the tomatoes, salt to taste, turmeric, coriander, chilli powder, aniseed, and garam masala and stir-fry until the oil floats to the top. Stir in the yogurt and mix well.
4. Add the fish steaks. Spoon the sauce over them, cover, and leave to cook on a low heat until tender. Turn the fish over halfway through cooking. Serve sprinkled with the chopped mint and coriander.

Serve with plain rice or a pulao.

Suitable for freezing if using fresh fish.

Muj Gard
(Radish Fish)
SERVES 4-6

*T*he combination of fish and white radish is characteristic of the unusual style of Kashmiri cooks. They are experts in bringing together atypical ingredients to prepare the most exotic and sumptuous feasts and this dish is no exception. The coarseness of the radish is tempered through cooking and the addition of spices and lemon juice enhances the flavours of the fish. Altogether an enjoyable dish both to prepare and to eat.

1kg (2 lb) any firm white fish, such as cod, in a piece
salt for rubbing
1-2 tablespoons lemon juice
4 large tomatoes and 1 tablespoon tomato purée or 4 large canned tomatoes, drained
1 teaspoon ground aniseed
$^1/_2$-1 teaspoon chilli powder
1 teaspoon garam masala
$^1/_2$ teaspoon ground turmeric
1-2 teaspoons ground coriander
$^1/_2$ teaspoon ground ginger
salt to taste
5-6 tablespoons ghee, mustard oil, or any other cooking oil
250g (8 oz) white radish (mooli)
250ml (8 fl oz) water
2 tablespoons fresh coriander leaves, chopped

Preparation time: 30 minutes
Cooking time: 30 minutes

1. Wash and slice the fish into steaks. Rub in the salt and lemon juice and leave to marinate for 30 minutes. Allow to drain in a colander.
2. In a food processor, blend together the tomatoes, aniseed, chilli powder, garam masala, turmeric, coriander, ginger and salt to taste.
3. Heat the ghee or oil in a frying pan. Shallow fry the fish on both sides. Remove from the pan and keep warm.
4. Cut the radish into 1cm ($^1/_2$ inch) slices. Fry in the same oil and set aside.
5. Using the same pan, add the tomato mixture, the fish steaks and the radish slices. Mix gently and add 250ml (8 fl oz) water and leave to simmer for 5-10 minutes. Serve sprinkled with the fresh coriander.

Serve with rice or Kashmiri Puri (p.92).

Unsuitable for freezing.

Muj Gard and Macchi Kebab (p.64).

Macchi Kebab
(Fish Kebabs)
SERVES 4-6

*F*or a snack these kebabs can be prepared without the sauce and deep-fried until *brown and cooked through. Serve with any chutney of your choice. Rose water is available from most Asian grocers.*

750g (1¹/₂ lb) fish, preferably cod

salt to taste

1 teaspoon chilli powder

¹/₂ teaspoon black cummin seeds, ground

1 teaspoon garam masala

1 large onion, finely chopped

1-2 tablespoons plain white flour

1 large egg

3 tablespoons almonds, blanched and ground

125ml (4 fl oz) natural yogurt, beaten

1 tablespoon rice flour

5-6 tablespoons ghee or oil

5-7 green cardamom pods, seeds removed

1 teaspoon ground aniseed or fennel

1 teaspoon ground coriander

¹/₂ teaspoon ground ginger

250ml (8 fl oz) water

1 tablespoon rose water (optional)

1-2 tablespoons fresh coriander leaves, finely chopped

Preparation time: 30 minutes
Cooking time: 1 hour 20 minutes

1. Wash, skin and cut the fish into small pieces. Place the fish in a metal colander or steamer, and then place this over a pan of boiling water. The water should reach just below the level of the colander. Cover and steam on a low heat until cooked.

2. Remove the fish and mash, adding salt to taste, chilli powder, ground black cummin seeds, garam masala, chopped onion, flour and egg. Mix well. Divide this mixture into 12. Dampen your hands with a little water and flatten each piece to make a small patty.

3. Grease the colander or steamer with ghee or oil, put in the kebabs and steam until firm. Remove and set aside for about 10-15 minutes.

4. Mix together the almonds and yogurt to make a fine paste. Add the rice flour.

5. Add the ghee or oil to a heavy-based pan. Add the cardamom seeds, the almond yogurt, aniseed, coriander, ginger, and salt to taste. Stir on a medium to low heat.

6. Add the kebabs and water. Bring to the boil. Lower the heat and simmer for about 10 minutes. Add the rose water, if liked. Serve sprinkled with the fresh coriander.

Serve with rice or Kashmiri Roti (p.88).

Unsuitable for freezing.

Macchi Dum Kashmiri
(Spicy Kashmiri Fish)
SERVES 4-6

A traditional Kashmiri fish dish cooked with yogurt and fragrant spices. Serve alongside Kabuli Channa Chawal (p.94), Marzwangan Korma (p.32) and Dhingri Chole (p.81) for a sumptuous feast.

1kg (2 lb) cod or any other firm
  fish fillets or steaks
salt for rubbing
$\frac{1}{2}$ teaspoon ground turmeric
5-6 tablespoons oil
a pinch asafoetida
1 teaspoon ground coriander
1 teaspoon cummin seeds
2.5cm (1 inch) piece fresh root
  ginger, ground to a paste
250ml (8 fl oz) natural yogurt,
  beaten
salt to taste
250ml (8 fl oz) water
1 teaspoon garam masala
4 green chillies (optional)
2 tablespoons fresh coriander,
  finely chopped

Preparation time: 15 minutes
Cooking time: 45 minutes

1. Wash and dry the fish and rub the pieces with a little salt and turmeric powder. Set aside. Heat the oil in a large frying pan. Fry the fish pieces lightly until golden. Drain on kitchen paper.
2. Using the same oil, add the asafoetida, coriander, cummin seeds, and ginger. As they begin to brown add the well-beaten yogurt and salt to taste. Cook over a low heat, stirring frequently until the colour turns to a reddish brown.
3. Add the fish pieces and 250ml (8 fl oz) water. Spoon the mixture over the fish. Cover and simmer on a low heat until the gravy thickens. This should take approximately 15 minutes. Take care not to break the fish pieces. If there is too much gravy then remove the fish, increase the heat and boil to reduce the gravy. Replace the fish in the sauce.
4. Add the garam masala, whole green chillies, and fresh coriander. Mix gently and cover. Allow to cook for 5 minutes.

Serve hot with rice or Kesar Mattar Pulao (p.101).

Unsuitable for freezing.

VEGETABLES AND VEGETARIAN DISHES

Nadhru
(Lotus Root)
SERVES 4

*F*resh lotus roots can be found in Asian or Chinese shops, however I find that the *canned lotus roots are more readily available and just as good. Once opened, canned lotus roots should be used straight away.*

400g (14 oz) fresh lotus root
  or 350g (12 oz) canned lotus
  root, drained
5-6 tablespoons oil
salt to taste
$^1/_4$ teaspoon chilli powder
$^1/_2$ teaspoon garam masala
1 teaspoon mango powder
  (amchoor)
$1^1/_2$ teaspoon ground coriander
2-3 tablespoons gram (chick-
  pea) flour
125ml (4 fl oz) water
2 tablespoons fresh coriander
  leaves, chopped
lemon wedges

Preparation time: 10 minutes (canned lotus root)
Cooking time: 15 minutes (canned lotus root)

1. If using fresh lotus root, scrape off the top skin and cut diagonally into 2.5cm (1 inch) slices. Wash thoroughly and boil in lightly salted water until tender. Drain.
2. Heat the oil in a non-stick frying pan. When hot add the fresh boiled or sliced canned lotus root and fry on a low heat until brown.
3. Add the salt, chilli powder, garam masala, mango powder, ground coriander and the flour and stir well. Add the water and mix well. Stir-fry so as to coat all the lotus root pieces. Cover and leave on a low heat for 2-3 minutes.
4. Serve garnished with the fresh coriander and lemon wedges.

Serve with Chapattis.

Unsuitable for freezing.

Previous pages: Mundiya (p.69), Nadhru and Karam Ka Saag (p.69).

Mundiya
(Kohlrabi)
SERVES 4-6

This is a quick and easy recipe to prepare. It has a spicy taste and can be eaten with a main meal or as a light lunch with rice.

4 tablespoons mustard oil
4-6 cloves garlic, finely
  chopped
500g (1 lb) kohlrabi peeled and
  cut into 2.5cm (1 inch) cubes
salt to taste
$\frac{1}{2}$ teaspoon chilli powder
1 teaspoon ground coriander
$\frac{1}{2}$ teaspoon ground turmeric
250-300ml (8-10 fl oz) water
$\frac{1}{2}$ teaspoon garam masala

Preparation time: 10 minutes
Cooking time: 25 minutes

1. Heat the oil in a heavy-based pan and allow it to smoke before lowering the heat as this will remove the pungency and give a sweet flavour.
2. Add the garlic and kohlrabi and sauté until pink in colour. Add the salt, chilli powder, coriander, and turmeric. Sauté for 1 minute and then pour in the water. Bring to the boil and simmer on low heat until the kohlrabi is tender. Mix in the garam masala and serve.

Karam Ka Saag
(Spring Greens)
SERVES 4

Although mustard greens are usually used in this recipe they are difficult to find in the UK so I have substituted spring greens.

6 tablespoons mustard oil
6-8 cloves garlic, peeled and
  chopped
3 whole dried red chillies and
  $\frac{1}{2}$ teaspoon chilli powder
750g (1$\frac{1}{2}$ lb) spring greens
  chopped into 2.5cm (1 inch)
  pieces
1$\frac{1}{2}$ teaspoons ground coriander
salt to taste
500ml (16 fl oz) water

Preparation time: 15 minutes
Cooking time: 30 minutes

1. Heat the mustard oil in a large pan and allow it to smoke before lowering the heat.
2. Add the garlic, whole red chillies, chilli powder, and the greens. Toss together for a few seconds. Add the ground coriander, salt and water. Allow to simmer for about 20 minutes, stirring from time to time until the greens are tender. There should be some liquid remaining at the end of cooking. Remove the whole chillies before serving.

Tsoont Waangan
(Aubergine with Apple)
SERVES 4-6

*I*n India, Kashmir is the home of apple orchards. Kashmiris expertly combine fruit and vegetables to make delectable meals and this particular recipe brings together the tartness of the Bramley apples with the discreet flavours of the aubergine.

3-4 Bramley or any other
  cooking apples
1kg (2 lb) aubergines
8 tablespoons mustard oil, any
  other oil, or ghee
a pinch of asafoetida
1 teaspoon cummin seeds,
  crushed
$\frac{1}{2}$ teaspoon aniseed or fennel
  seeds, crushed
$\frac{1}{2}$ teaspoon ground turmeric
$\frac{1}{2}$ teaspoon chilli powder
1 teaspoon paprika
salt to taste
1 tablespoon fresh coriander
  leaves, chopped

Preparation time: 15 minutes
Cooking time: 35 minutes

1. Wash, core and cut each apple into 6 thick wedges.
2. Wash and cut the aubergines into 2.5cm (1 inch) thick slices. If using fat aubergines then cut them in half lengthwise and then slice into 2.5cm (1 inch) pieces.
3. Heat the mustard oil and let it come to smoking point to take away the pungency. Allow to cool slightly then fry the apple wedges on both sides until golden brown. Remove from the oil and put in a colander to drain.
4. In the same oil fry the aubergine slices a few at a time until golden brown on both sides. When removing the aubergines from the oil squeeze the slices in a draining spoon to remove any excess oil. Put them aside with the apples.
5. In the same pan add the asafoetida, crushed cummin and aniseed, turmeric, chilli, and paprika. Stir and then add the aubergine and apple slices and stir-fry gently. Add the salt to taste and reduce the heat.
6. Before serving remove the excess oil with a spoon and sprinkle with the fresh coriander.

Serve hot with any Kashmiri bread.

Unsuitable for freezing.

Bhare Karela (p.72) and Tsoont Waangan.

Bhare Karela
(Bitter Gourd)
SERVES 4

*O*ne *of the more unusual vegetables, Karela, or bitter gourd, has a sharp but distinctive flavour and is available from most Asian stores.*

10 medium-size bitter gourds
  (karela)
$1/2$ teaspoon salt
$1/2$ teaspoon ground turmeric

Filling:
oil for deep-frying
1 medium onion, diced
4 medium potatoes, peeled and
  cubed
3 tablespoons oil
1 teaspoon ground coriander
2 teaspoons dried mango
  powder (amchoor)
$1/2$ teaspoon garam masala
1 teaspoon ground cummin
1cm ($1/2$ inch) piece fresh root
  ginger, peeled and grated
$1/4$ teaspoon dried mint leaves or
  1 tablespoon fresh mint,
  finely chopped
1 teaspoon salt or to taste

Preparation time: 1 hour 15 minutes
Cooking time: 45 minutes

1. Scrape the outer skin of the bitter gourds and slit them lengthwise. Scoop out the seeds and pulp. Retain the tender pulp for the filling and discard the seeds. Rub the salt and turmeric into the slits and all over the bitter gourds and put aside for 1 hour. At the end of this time, gently squeeze out the water from the bitter gourds.

2. Heat the oil for frying in a wok or deep frying pan and fry the onion until golden brown. Remove the onion from the oil, drain and set aside.

3. In the same oil fry the potatoes until tender and golden brown. Remove, drain and set aside.

4. Heat the 3 tablespoons oil in a non-stick frying pan and fry the bitter gourd pulp for a few minutes.

5. Mix the onion, potatoes and fried bitter gourd purée with the remaining filling ingredients and use this mixture to stuff the whole bitter gourds. Secure tightly with thread and then deep-fry until golden brown.

6. Fry all the bitter gourds in the same way. Drain out the oil and return the fried bitter gourds to the non-stick frying pan, adding 3-4 tablespoons of water. Cover and simmer on low heat for 15-20 minutes until they are tender. Remove the threads before serving.

Serve hot with Chapattis.

Unsuitable for freezing.

Malai Shalgam
(Turnips in Cream Sauce)
SERVES 4-6

This enticing recipe has been created in a land where the summer vegetables contain an almost sweet essence. The Kashmiris have a way of turning a modest vegetable such as the turnip into a dish worthy of any banquet.

1kg (2 lb) young and tender
   turnips
2 medium onions, peeled and
   roughly chopped
4-5 cloves garlic, peeled
2.5cm (1 inch) piece fresh root
   ginger, peeled
60ml (2 fl oz) oil
1 teaspoon ground coriander
1 teaspoon ground cummin
$^1/_2$ teaspoon garam masala
$^1/_2$ teaspoon chilli powder
$^1/_2$ teaspoon ground aniseed
$^1/_2$ teaspoon paprika
salt and black pepper to taste
4 tablespoons natural yogurt,
   beaten
350ml (12 fl oz) water
60ml (2 fl oz) double cream
3 tablespoons fresh coriander
   leaves, chopped

Preparation time: 15 minutes
Cooking time: 30 minutes

1. Wash, peel and cut the turnips into small 1cm ($^1/_2$ inch) cubes.
2. Purée, in a blender, the onion, garlic and ginger.
3. In a heavy-based pan heat the oil, add the onion purée and stir-fry for 3 minutes until it slightly changes colour.
4. Add the diced turnips, all the spices and the salt and black pepper and stir-fry for 10 minutes on a low heat until the moisture evaporates. Take extra care not to burn the turnips.
5. Add the beaten yogurt and the water to the turnips. Lower the heat and simmer for about 10 minutes, until the gravy thickens and the turnips are tender.
6. Stir in the cream and the fresh coriander. Cover and leave to simmer for 10 minutes.

Serve with rice or Kashmiri Roti (p.88).

Unsuitable for freezing.

Gobi Dum
(Cauliflower)
SERVES 4-6

This is a common dish prepared in most Kashmiri households. Kashmiri vegetables grow in plenty during the summer months and it is simple but tasty dishes like this that provide most Kashmiri homes with their staple diet.

1kg (2 lb) cauliflower
5 tablespoons ghee, mustard oil
  or any other cooking oil
a pinch of asafoetida
1 teaspoon cummin seeds
salt to taste
1/2 teaspoon chilli powder
2.5cm (1 inch) piece fresh root
  ginger, peeled and cut into
  slivers
1/2 teaspoon ground turmeric
1 1/2 teaspoons ground coriander
1/2 teaspoon garam masala
1 tablespoon lemon juice
2 tablespoons natural yogurt,
  (optional)
2 tablespoons fresh coriander
  leaves, finely chopped

Preparation time: 15 minutes
Cooking time: 25 minutes

1. Wash and cut the cauliflower into small florets with long, thin stems.
2. Heat the ghee or oil in a wok or a non-stick frying pan. If using mustard oil, heat to smoking point, then reduce the heat. This takes away the pungency and gives the oil a sweet flavour. Add the asafoetida and cummin seeds. Fry for 20 seconds and then add the cauliflower florets and cover tightly and leave for 1-2 minutes.
3. Remove the lid and stir-fry again for 1-2 minutes. Cover tightly and leave on a medium heat for a further 1-2 minutes. The cauliflower should now have a brownish appearance. Repeat this process until the cauliflower is a golden brown, taking care not to burn it.
4. Lower the heat, add the salt, chilli powder, ginger, turmeric, coriander, garam masala, lemon juice and yogurt, if used. Mix well, cover tightly and cook on a low heat until the cauliflower is tender, about 10-15 minutes. Serve sprinkled with the fresh coriander.

Serve with any rice or Indian bread.

Suitable for freezing.

Haak Saag (p.76) and Gobi Dum with lime and chilli chutney.

Haak Saag
(Spinach)
SERVES 4-6

The Kashmiris use a variety of greens in their cuisine. Most of these are particular to Kashmir alone and are not readily available elsewhere. Here, I have substituted spinach to make a delicious and nutritious dish.

1kg (2 lb) fresh spinach,
  washed and dried
5 tablespoons mustard oil or
  any other cooking oil
a pinch of asafoetida
$1/2$ teaspoon bicarbonate of
  soda
1 green chilli, chopped
  (optional)
salt to taste
$1/2$ teaspoon ground turmeric
1 teaspoon chilli powder
$1^1/2$ teaspoons ground coriander
$1/4$ teaspoon garam masala

Preparation time: 15 minutes
Cooking time: 20 minutes

1. Cut the spinach into 2.5cm (1 inch) pieces.
2. Heat the oil in a wok or deep frying pan. If using mustard oil, heat to smoking point and then lower the heat as this will take away the pungency and makes the oil sweeter.
3. Add the asafoetida, the spinach, bicarbonate of soda and green chilli and mix well. Add the salt, turmeric, chilli powder, and coriander and keep stirring until the spinach is cooked and the liquid has evaporated.
4. Mash the spinach mixture with the back of a spoon or a potato masher and then cook uncovered for a further 5-10 minutes until all the liquid has evaporated.
5. Sprinkle with the garam masala just before serving.

Serve hot with rice or bread or to accompany any main meal.

Suitable for freezing.

Dum Aloo
(Kashmiri Fried Potatoes)
SERVES 4-6

*T*here are many recipes for Dum Aloo. The curries prepared by the Kashmiri technique are very rich as the gravy consists mostly of ghee. If you wish you can add 250ml (8 fl oz) natural yogurt and some roasted cashew nuts to this recipe to make it even more delicious.

1kg (2 lb) small potatoes
mustard oil for frying
2-4 tablespoons ghee or oil
3-4 whole cloves
1 teaspoon chilli powder
2 teaspoons paprika
4 teaspoons ground coriander
3 green chillies, finely sliced
  (optional)
500ml (16 fl oz) water
salt to taste
5cm (2 inch) piece fresh root
  ginger, peeled and slivered
1 teaspoon Kashmiri garam
  masala, (see page 9)
4-5 tablespoons fresh coriander
  leaves, chopped

Preparation time: 10 minutes
Cooking time: 45 minutes

1. Wash the potatoes and boil them in water until they are $^3/_4$ cooked. Allow them to cool and then prick them all over with a fork.
2. Heat the mustard oil in a deep pan until smoking hot to take away the pungency. Allow to cool slightly and then fry the potatoes until golden brown. Remove them from the oil, drain and put to one side.
3. Heat the ghee or oil in a heavy-based frying pan. When the ghee is hot, reduce the heat and add the cloves, chilli powder, paprika, coriander, and green chillies, if used. Stir-fry for 1-2 minutes and add the water. Boil for 2-3 minutes.
4. Add the potatoes and salt to taste and leave to simmer, covered, on low until the potatoes are cooked and the water has almost all evaporated.
5. Add the ginger, garam masala and the fresh coriander. Cover tightly and leave for a few minutes before serving.

Serve with Kashmiri Puri (p.92).

Unsuitable for freezing.

Manakke Aur Khajoor Ki Tikkhi
(Dried Fruit Curry)
SERVES 4

In Kashmir the summer months bring a blaze of flourishing orchards and fruit gardens. Much of this produce is dried and stored away for the cold winter months. It is these dried delicacies that provide the ingredients for this dish. Its sweet and sour flavours and nutty texture tastes great at any time of year, and it is often eaten as an accompaniment to meat dishes such as Rogan Josh.

1 medium onion, chopped

3 tomatoes, chopped

5 cloves garlic, peeled

2.5cm (1 inch) piece fresh root ginger, peeled

1 teaspoon cummin seeds

4 tablespoons oil

1 teaspoon ground turmeric

1/2 -1 teaspoon chilli powder

1 teaspoon garam masala

1 teaspoon dried mango powder (amchoor)

2 teaspoons demerara sugar or jaggery

salt to taste

300ml (1/2 pint) water

125g (4 oz) dried dates, stoned and washed

15-20 unsalted cashew nuts, halved

60g (2 oz) raisins, soaked in water

1 tablespoon lemon juice (optional)

2-3 tablespoons fresh coriander leaves, chopped

Preparation time: 30 minutes

Cooking time: 45 minutes

1. In a blender, grind to a paste the onion, tomatoes, garlic, ginger, and cummin seeds.
2. Heat the oil in a pan and add to it the onion/tomato paste. Brown well until the oil separates from the paste.
3. Add the turmeric, chilli powder, garam masala, dried mango powder, demerara sugar, salt and water.
4. Add the dates, cashew nuts, raisins and lemon juice, if used. Simmer until the gravy is smooth and the nuts are soft.
5. Serve garnished with the fresh coriander.

Serve hot with rice or Chapattis.

Suitable for freezing.

Manakke Aur Khajoor Ki Tikkhi.

Mandira
(Black Lentils)
SERVES 4-6

*L*entils are a staple food in India and highly nutritious, especially black lentils. Kashmiris use mustard oil for this particular recipe as it gives it that extra special flavour, however any other oil can be substituted. For a more exotic taste mix 250ml (8 fl oz) single cream with 250ml (8 fl oz) yogurt and 60g (2 oz) raisins and add instead of the yogurt.

400g (14 oz) black urad dal, (whole black lentils)
6 tablespoons mustard oil or any other oil
a pinch of asafoetida
1 tablespoon whole cummin seeds
2 medium onions, sliced
4-6 cloves garlic, minced
2.5cm (1 inch) piece fresh root ginger, peeled and grated
2 tablespoons tomato purée
1 teaspoon ground coriander
1/2 teaspoon chilli powder
2 green chillies, chopped (optional)
salt to taste
500ml (16 fl oz) natural yogurt, beaten well

Preparation time: 30 minutes plus 4-6 hours soaking time
Cooking time: 1 hour

1. Wash and soak the dal for 4-6 hours. Drain and boil the dal in lightly salted water with 1 tablespoon oil, until tender. Drain and reserve the cooking liquid.
2. Heat the mustard oil in a heavy-based pan on a medium heat and allow to smoke for a few seconds. Reduce the heat and allow to cool slightly. (If using other oils, just heat in the usual way.)
3. Add the asafoetida, cummin seeds, sliced onions, garlic and ginger and stir-fry for 4-5 minutes. Add the tomato purée, coriander, chilli powder and green chillies, if used, and continue stir-frying for a few minutes.
4. Add the drained dal and salt to taste to the mixture. Stir in the yogurt and enough of the reserved cooking liquid to make a smooth sauce. Cook on a low heat for 15-20 minutes until the mixture is thoroughly blended.

Serve hot with any Kashmiri bread.

Suitable for freezing.

Dhingri Chole
(Dry White Mushrooms with Chick-peas)
SERVES 4-6

*T*he forests of Kashmir are carpeted with fields of fat juicy mushrooms and morels. Dhingri is a dried mushroom and the taste is incredible. It is very expensive and is used on special occasions. I have used Chinese dried mushrooms as a substitute, which are readily available from most Oriental grocers.

625g (1¼ lb) canned chick-peas, drained or 200g (7 oz) dried chick-peas, soaked overnight

salt to taste

½ teaspoon bicarbonate of soda

10 Chinese dried mushrooms

500ml (16 fl oz) water, for soaking mushrooms

5 tablespoons ghee or oil

2 bunches spring onions, approx. 180-200g (6-7 oz), finely chopped

6 cloves garlic, peeled and ground to a paste

5cm (2 inch) piece fresh root ginger, peeled and ground to a paste

3 large tomatoes, chopped

1 teaspoon ground turmeric

2-3 tablespoons lemon juice

2 teaspoons cummin seeds

1 teaspoon garam masala

½ teaspoon chilli powder

½ teaspoon freshly ground black pepper

1 teaspoon ground cummin

250ml (8 fl oz) water

3 tablespoons fresh coriander leaves

Preparation time: 20 minutes (canned chick-peas) or overnight (raw chick-peas)
Cooking time: 45 minutes

1. If using soaked chick-peas, drain them and cook with a little salt, ½ teaspoon bicarbonate of soda and water in a pressure cooker for 25 minutes or alternatively in a covered pan until soft. Drain.
2. Soak the Chinese mushrooms in the water for about 20 minutes and then boil for five minutes. Drain and mince coarsely.
3. Heat the oil in a frying pan and fry the spring onions until brown. Add the garlic and ginger, and fry for a few minutes. Add the tomatoes, turmeric, lemon juice, cummin seeds, garam masala, chilli powder, black pepper and ground cummin and stir-fry until the oil comes to the surface.
4. Add the mushrooms and stir-fry for 1 minute. Add the chick-peas and salt to taste and continue stir-frying. Lower the heat, add the water and simmer, tightly covered, for 10 minutes. Sprinkle with the fresh coriander and serve.

Serve with Kashmiri Naan.

Unsuitable for freezing.

Kadhi Kashmiri
(Gram Flour Dumplings in a Yogurt Sauce)
SERVES 4-5

*T*his recipe is a Kashmiri version of Kadhai. Mustard oil and asafoetida give it a distinctive flavour.

For the Pakoras:

150g (5 oz) gram (chick-pea) flour

salt to taste

$1/4$ -$1/2$ teaspoon chilli powder

$1/4$ -$1/2$ teaspoon whole cummin seeds

a pinch of bicarbonate of soda

a pinch of asafoetida, mixed with a little water

about 125ml (4 fl oz) warm water for mixing

oil or mustard oil for frying

For the Kadhi:

60ml (2 fl oz) natural yogurt, mixed with 500ml (16 fl oz) water

30g (1 oz) gram (chick-pea) flour

1 teaspoon salt or to taste

$1/2$ teaspoon chilli powder

$1/2$ teaspoon ground turmeric

1 litre (32 fl oz) water

1 tablespoon oil or mustard oil

a pinch of asafoetida

1 teaspoon cummin seeds

1 teaspoon sugar

1 tablespoon fresh mint leaves, chopped

2 green chillies, deseeded and chopped

Preparation time: 30 minutes
Cooking time: 50 minutes

1. To make the pakoras, mix the gram flour with the salt, chilli powder, cummin seeds, bicarbonate of soda and asafoetida water. Add warm water and mix well until it forms a thick batter.
2. Heat the oil in a wok or deep frying pan. If using mustard oil, heat the oil to smoking point to eliminate the pungency and retain a sweet flavour. Allow to cool and deep fry marble-sized pieces of pakora batter, on a medium heat, until golden brown. Drain on kitchen paper and set aside.
3. For the Kadhi, mix the yogurt-water with the gram flour, whisking well to make sure that there are no lumps. Add the salt, chilli powder, turmeric, and water and whisk well.
4. Heat the oil, add the asafoetida, cummin seeds and the yogurt-water mixture and continue whisking until it starts to boil. Cover and leave on a low heat to simmer for 20 minutes, stirring occasionally.
5. Add the sugar, mint and green chillies and cook for 10 minutes. The consistency should be like a thick soup. Stir in the pakoras and simmer on a low heat until the pakoras are soft.

Serve with white rice.

Unsuitable for freezing.

Kadhi Kashmiri with Basmati rice.

Gucchi Chamon
(Cheese Morel Curry)
SERVES 4-6

*T*his *exclusive dish is served in Kashmir mostly on special occasions. However, it is truly 'Once eaten, never forgotten'. Traditionally 'RatanJot ' (a plant found in the Western Himalayas) was used to give this sumptuous dish a wonderful red colour. As morels are expensive other varieties of mushroom can be substituted. If using other mushrooms increase the quantity as the morels are dry and swell up on cooking.*

90g (3 oz) dried morels

250ml (8 fl oz) ghee or oil

250g (8 oz) paneer (see page 9),
　　cut into cubes

1cm (¹/₂ inch) fresh root ginger,
　　peeled and ground to a paste

1 tablespoon poppy seeds,
　　ground to a paste

2 tablespoons almonds,
　　blanched and ground to a
　　paste

¹/₂ teaspoon ground cummin
　　seeds

¹/₂ teaspoon ground aniseed

6 medium tomatoes, skinned
　　and finely chopped

1 teaspoon sugar

salt to taste

1 teaspoon chilli powder

1 teaspoon paprika

1 teaspoon garam masala

500ml (16 fl oz) natural yogurt,
　　beaten

Preparation time: 1 hour
Cooking Time: 35-45 minutes

1. Soak the morels in hot water for 1 hour.
2. Heat the oil or ghee in a heavy-based saucepan on a high heat and fry the paneer cubes in small batches until light brown in colour. Drain on kitchen paper.
3. In the same saucepan add the ginger, poppy seed and almond pastes and sauté for 30 seconds. Add the ground cummin seed, aniseed and the finely chopped tomatoes. Leave to simmer for 10 minutes or until the sauce has a smooth texture. You can use a potato masher to make the sauce smooth.
4. Squeeze the water from the morels and add them to the sauce. Stir-fry for 2-3 minutes and then add the sugar, salt, chilli powder, paprika and the garam masala and cook for a further 5 minutes.
5. Add the paneer and allow to simmer for 8-10 minutes. Add the yogurt and cook on a low heat to prevent the yogurt from curdling. When heated through, serve at once.

Serve with rice or any Kashmiri bread.

Unsuitable for freezing.

Mehti Chamon
(Indian Cheese with Spinach and Fenugreek)
SERVES 4-6

*W*hen making the paneer for this recipe, keep the excess water (whey) and use when preparing the gravy. Instead of using paneer you can use cooked potato or boiled or canned lotus root, cut into small cubes.

350g (12 oz) pressed paneer
  (see page 9)
mustard oil or any other oil for
  frying
180g (6 oz) fenugreek leaves,
  washed and chopped
400g (14 oz) fresh spinach,
  washed and chopped
125ml (4 fl oz) ghee or oil
500ml (16 fl oz) paneer whey
  or water
salt to taste
1 teaspoon ground turmeric
4 teaspoons ground coriander
1 teaspoon chilli powder
30g (1 oz) fresh root ginger,
  peeled and grated
1 teaspoon Kashmiri garam
  masala, (see page 9)
a little lemon juice

Preparation time: 1 hour
Cooking time: 45 minutes

1. Cut the paneer into long strips and then into diamond shapes. Set aside.
2. Heat the mustard oil to smoking point to eliminate the pungent taste, allow to cool slightly and fry the paneer until golden brown. Remove and drain.
3. Put the fenugreek and spinach in a blender and purée with a little whey or water.
4. Heat the ghee or oil in a heavy-based frying pan. Add the spinach and fenugreek purée and keep stirring on a medium heat until all the moisture evaporates and the oil separates out.
5. Add 125ml (4 fl oz) whey, salt to taste, turmeric, coriander and chilli powder and stir-fry for 2-5 minutes until the oil separates and no liquid remains.
6. Add the fried paneer to the mixture together with the ginger, Kashmiri garam masala and the remaining whey. Cover tightly and simmer on a low heat for 10-15 minutes. The ghee should float to the top and the dish is ready. Add a little lemon juice for extra taste.

Serve hot with plain white rice.

Unsuitable for freezing.

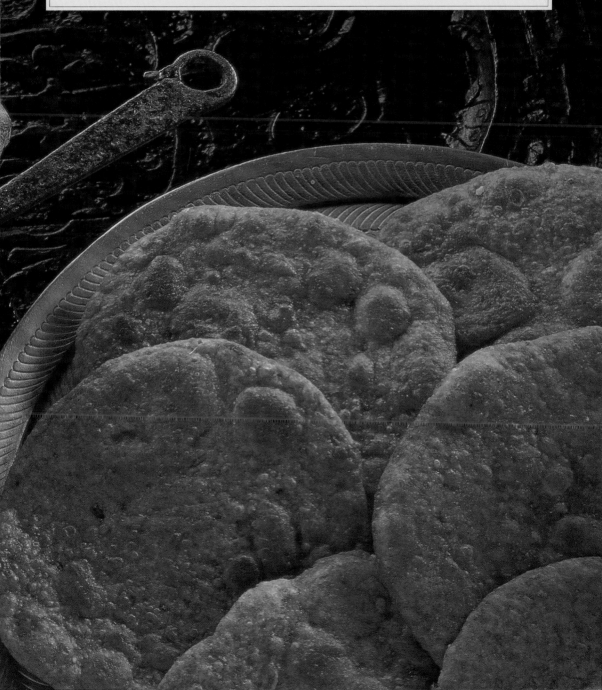

BREADS AND RICE

Kashmiri Roti

MAKES 10

A substitute for the everyday chapatti or phulka, Kashmiri Roti are eaten in most households. The spices add flavour and this roti tastes particularly nice on its own.

500g (1 lb) wholewheat flour
  (medium ground)
1 teaspoon salt
1 teaspoon ground black
  pepper
$^1/_2$ teaspoon aniseed
$^1/_2$ teaspoon cummin seeds
a pinch of asafoetida
a pinch of carum seeds (ajwain)
warm milk for kneading
oil or ghee for shallow frying

Preparation time: 30 minutes
Cooking time: 30 minutes

1. Mix the flour with the salt. Add the black pepper, aniseed, cummin seeds, asafoetida and carum seeds. Slowly pour in enough warm milk to make a stiff dough and knead together. Sprinkle in a little water if the dough becomes too stiff.
2. Divide the dough into 10 portions and roll out each portion into a disc about 7.5-10cm (3-4 inch) in diameter and 0.5cm ($^1/_4$ inch) thick.
3. Prick the roti lightly with a fork. Cook on a lightly oiled hot griddle or heavy-based frying pan, over a low heat. Turn frequently, adding around 1-2 teaspoons oil to the pan while cooking. Cook until both sides of the roti are golden brown.

Serve hot with any main dish or starter, or on their own with yogurt.

Unsuitable for freezing

Previous pages: Roghani Roti (p.89), Chapattis (p.93) and Kashmiri roti.

Roghani Roti

MAKES 8

*A*nother variation of the traditional roti. The combination of white flour and wholewheat flour makes a flakier, more biscuit-like bread.

500g (1 lb) wholewheat flour or 250g (8 oz) wholewheat flour mixed with 250g (8 oz) plain white flour
salt to taste
4 tablespoons melted butter or single cream
Approx. 180ml (6 fl oz) warm milk
4 strands saffron, soaked in 1 tablespoon milk
ghee or oil for frying

Preparation time: 1 hour
Cooking time: 20 minutes

1. Mix the flour and salt together. Add the melted butter or cream.
2. Stir in enough warm milk to make into a soft but not sticky dough. Cover and put to one side for 30 minutes.
3. Knead the dough and divide it into 8 portions. Shape into balls.
4. On a lightly floured surface, roll each ball into a 15cm (6 inch) diameter disc. Brush the top of each roti with a little saffron milk.
5. Heat a griddle or heavy-based frying pan on a high heat, then lower the heat to medium to low. Brush the pan with a little ghee or oil and fry the roti on both sides until golden brown. Each side should take about 3-4 minutes to brown. Repeat the process until all the rotis are cooked.

Unsuitable for freezing.

Sheermal

MAKES 12

*K*ashmiri Muslims make a wide variety of unleavened breads. Sheermal is sprinkled with saffron flavoured milk to keep it moist and add a little natural colour. This bread is best served with kebabs, meat dishes or vegetables. Leftover rotis are eaten with pickle, as a light snack or with tea.

2 teaspoons sugar
375ml (12 fl oz) milk
1 teaspoon saffron
625g (1¼ lb) plain flour
a pinch of salt
1-2 eggs, beaten
Approx. 250ml (8 fl oz) ghee or
  clarified butter, melted
flour for sprinkling
ghee or butter for brushing

Preparation time: 30 minutes plus 1-2 hours resting
Cooking time: 9-10 minutes

1. Dissolve the sugar in 300ml (½ pint) warm milk. Add the saffron to the remaining milk and set aside.
2. Sieve the flour and salt together. Make a well in the centre of the flour, add the eggs and gradually pour in enough of the sugar milk to mix to a soft but not sticky dough. If you use 2 eggs you will need less milk. Knead the dough until smooth. Cover with a dampened cloth and set aside for 1-2 hours.
3. Gradually add the melted ghee to the dough and knead well until all the ghee has been absorbed. Cover and set aside for another 10-20 minutes.
4. Divide the dough into 12 balls. Cover with a dampened cloth and set aside for 10-15 minutes. Preheat the oven to 180°C, 350°F, Gas Mark 4.
5. Roll out the balls, on a lightly floured surface, into 18cm (7 inch) diameter discs. Prick them all over with a fork.
6. Put the Sheermal on to lightly greased baking trays. Bake in the oven for 4-5 minutes. Remove and brush with the saffron-milk mixture and bake for further 4 minutes until brown.
7. Brush the Sheermal with ghee or butter as soon as they come out of the oven, and serve.

Unsuitable for freezing.

Sheermal and Kashmiri Puri (p.92).

Kashmiri Puri
MAKES 15-20

*P*uris are made throughout India but it is the addition of aniseed that makes this dish distinctively Kashmiri. This is a great favourite with my family as it has an unusual but delectable taste not found in other puris.

1 teaspoon dried yeast
2 teaspoons sugar
125ml (4 fl oz) warm milk
125g (4 oz) fine wholewheat flour
125g (4 oz) plain white flour
a pinch of salt
1 tablespoon aniseed, roasted and ground
8 strands saffron, soaked in 1 tablespoon warm milk
2 tablespoons natural yogurt
1 teaspoon poppy seeds
ghee or oil for frying

Preparation time: 20 minutes plus 4-6 hours resting
Cooking time: 30 minutes

1. Sprinkle the yeast and 1 teaspoon sugar over the warm milk. Cover and leave aside until frothy.
2. Sieve together the wholewheat and plain flours and salt into a bowl. Add the remaining sugar and the aniseed. Gradually pour in the yeast mixture. Add extra milk if necessary to mix to a soft dough. Mix well and knead the dough until smooth. Cover with a damp cloth and leave, in a warm place, for 4-6 hours or preferably overnight.
3. The next morning, knead again. Divide the dough into 15-20 portions and shape these into balls.
4. On a lightly floured board, roll out each ball into a 10cm (4 inch) diameter round disc.
5. Mix the saffron milk, yogurt and poppy seeds together and leave aside for 15 minutes.
6. Heat the ghee or oil in a deep frying pan and lower the heat to medium. Smear both sides of the puris with the saffron mixture. Slide the puris into the hot oil, press the puri down gently with a slotted spoon until the puri puffs up. Turn over and fry until golden brown. Do not fry more than 2 puris at a time. Drain on kitchen paper.

Unsuitable for freezing.

Chapatti Or Phulka

MAKES 4-6

Phulka or chapatti is eaten daily in most Indian households. The difference between phulka and chapatti is that phulka means 'puffed' and has been derived from the Hindi 'phulna' to swell. Chapatti, however is derived from 'chapta' and relates to a flatter bread. In both cases the dough is the same. Making good phulka takes a lot of practise and is an acquired art.

250g (8 oz) fine wholewheat
  flour
½ teaspoon salt or to taste
125ml (4 fl oz) water
flour for dusting

Preparation time: 30 minutes plus 30 minutes resting
Cooking time: 15 minutes

1. Mix together the flour and salt to taste. Mix to a dough by adding water, a little at a time, to the flour. The dough is usually kneaded with knuckles as this gives a more smooth and pliable mixture. Cover and leave the dough for 30 minutes.
2. Knead again. Shape the dough into balls about the size of golf balls. On a lightly floured board roll out the balls into thin discs of about 13cm (5 inch) in diameter.
3. Heat a griddle or heavy-based frying pan on a medium heat.
4. To make phulka, place the dough disc on the heated griddle and brown lightly on both sides. Once both sides have browned, the phulka is quickly removed and is placed directly over a flame or alternatively put under a very hot grill to puff up. Turn the phulka over using tongs. Serve straight away.
5. Alternatively a chapatti can be cooked on the griddle on a medium heat. Place the chapatti on the griddle and after about 30 seconds turn over and cook the other side. Remove from the griddle once browned and brush a little ghee or oil on top before serving. Serve hot.

Unsuitable for freezing.

Kabuli Channa Chawal
(Chick-pea Pulao)
SERVES 4-6

*A*n exotic mixture of nuts, raisins and chick-peas, this pulao is a wonderfully fragrant dish with a nutty texture. It is very versatile and can be eaten alongside virtually any other dish. Try it with some plain fresh yogurt for a healthy and delicious lunch. I have used dried chick-peas in this recipe but canned chick-peas can be used for quick and convenient cooking.

300g (10 oz) dried chick-peas
a pinch bicarbonate of soda
400g (14 oz) Basmati rice
4 tablespoons ghee or oil
2 medium onions, finely sliced
60g (2 oz) almonds, blanched
   and slivered
1 tablespoon shelled pistachio
   nuts
2 tablespoons raisins
2 whole cloves
2 green cardamom pods
2 bay leaves
6 black peppercorns
2.5cm (1 inch) cinnamon stick
salt to taste
1/2 teaspoon chilli powder
1 litre (32 fl oz) water

Preparation time: 30 minutes plus soaking time
Cooking time: 30 minutes

1. Soak the chick-peas overnight in cold water with a pinch of bicarbonate of soda. The following day boil them for 30 minutes or until soft. Alternatively use drained canned chick-peas.
2. Wash and soak the rice for 20-30 minutes. Drain.
3. Put the oil or ghee in a heavy-based pan and fry the onion slices until golden brown and crisp. Drain and set aside. In the same oil fry the nuts and raisins, drain and set aside.
4. To the same oil add all the whole spices. Stir-fry for 1-2 minutes then add the rice, salt, chilli powder, and water. Cover tightly and simmer for 15 minutes on a low heat or until the rice is cooked.
5. Mix in the chick-peas, cover tightly and leave on low for 10-15 minutes until cooked through.
6. Garnish with the fried onions, nuts and raisins.

Unsuitable for freezing.

Kabuli Channa Chawal.

Emperors Kashmiri Biryani
SERVES 4-6

Biriyanis are another Wazawaan (celebratory banquet) speciality. This Biryani is an age-old recipe from the Vale of Kashmir dating from the reign of Shahjahan.

1kg (2-2¼ lb) chicken, with
  giblets, skinned and cut into
  8-10 pieces
water
30g (1 oz) shelled pistachios
2 teaspoons fennel seeds
2 teaspoons cummin seeds
1 teaspoon paprika
1 tablespoon garam masala
60ml (2 fl oz) natural yogurt
5 tablespoons ghee or oil
2 large onions, peeled and
  finely chopped
15-20 almonds, blanched
125g (4 oz) raisins
5-6 whole cloves
3 brown cardamom pods
Two 5cm (2 inch) cinnamon
  sticks
2 bay leaves
10-12 black peppercorns
4 cloves garlic, finely chopped
salt to taste
2-3 tablespoons fresh mint
  leaves
500g (1 lb) Basmati Rice
2 litres (3½ pints) water
1 teaspoon saffron, soaked in
  60ml (2 fl oz) hot milk

Preparation time: 45 minutes
Cooking time: 2 hours

1. Boil the chicken neck, wings and giblets with 350ml (12 fl oz) water to make 250ml (8 fl oz) of stock.
2. Grind together the pistachios, fennel, cummin, paprika and garam masala. Mix with the yogurt.
3. Heat the ghee or oil in a large saucepan. Add half the onion and fry until brown. Remove and drain. In the same oil fry the almonds and raisins until the almonds become golden brown and the raisins puff up. Remove and drain.
4. To the same oil add the cloves, cardamoms, cinnamon, bay leaves, and peppercorns and fry for 1-2 minutes. Add the remaining onion and the garlic and fry until brown. Add the pistachio paste, stirring constantly.
5. Add the chicken and salt and fry for a minute. Add the strained stock and mix well. Cover and cook for 15 minutes, stirring occasionally. Stir in the fresh mint leaves, cover and cook until the chicken is tender.
6. Meanwhile, boil the rice in the water with 1 tablespoon oil, until half-cooked. Drain.
7. Spread the chicken in the bottom of a casserole dish and cover with the rice. Sprinkle with the almonds, fried onions and raisins. Pour on the saffron mixture. Cover tightly and simmer on a low heat or alternatively bake in a preheated oven at 150°C, 300°F, Gas Mark 2 for 15-20 minutes or until the rice and chicken are cooked. Turn off the heat and leave for 5 minutes before serving.

Suitable for freezing.

Sada Chawal
(Plain Basmati Rice)
SERVES 4-6

White rice is usually eaten at all mealtimes and is a staple food throughout India. It is the particular flavour of the Basmati rice that gives such a distinctive aroma. Below are two methods of cooking Basmati Rice.

500g (1 lb) Basmati Rice
2 litres (3$\frac{1}{2}$ pints) water for method 1
or
Approx. 1 litre (1$\frac{3}{4}$ pints) hot water for method 2
2 tablespoons ghee or oil
salt to taste

Method 1
1. Soak the rice in cold water for about 15-20 minutes.
2. Wash the rice, 2-3 times in cold water.
3. Boil 2 litres (3$\frac{1}{2}$ pints) water in a pan over a high heat. Reduce the heat and add 1 teaspoon oil to help keep the rice grains separate and prevent them sticking. Add the rice and salt and boil for 5 minutes or until the rice is $\frac{3}{4}$ cooked.
4. Drain the rice in a colander and run some cold water over it for a few seconds. Allow to drain well.
5. Put the rice back into the clean pan and cover tightly. Cook over a very low heat for a further 10 minutes until the rice is cooked and fluffy. In a small pan, heat the remaining oil and pour over the cooked rice.

Method 2
1. Soak and wash and drain the rice as in Method 1
2. Heat 2 tablespoons oil in a heavy-based pan. When the oil is hot add the rice and stir for a few seconds to coat the rice. Add salt to taste.
3. Add enough hot water to come 2.5cm (1 inch) above the level of the rice. Alternatively use double the quantity of water to rice.
4. Bring to the boil, cover tightly and then leave to cook on a low heat for about 20 minutes or until the rice is cooked. Try not to open the pan during cooking. Gently stir the rice with a fork and serve.

Unsuitable for freezing.

Gucchi Pulao
(Mushroom or Morel Rice)
SERVES 4-6

*K*ashmir is noted for its different varieties of mushroom. The upland forests of Kishtwar are carpeted with juicy morels. In Kashmir morels are used to prepare this festive dish but I have used ordinary mushrooms in this recipe. If morels are available, reduce the quantity used.

500g (1 lb) Basmati rice
4-5 tablespoons ghee or oil
2 medium onions, sliced
2 brown cardamom pods
2.5cm (1 inch) cinnamon stick
2 bay leaves
250g (8 oz) mushrooms,
    washed and sliced or 200g
    (7 oz) sliced mushrooms and
    30g (1 oz) morels, soaked
$\frac{1}{2}$-1 teaspoon chilli powder
1 teaspoon ground coriander
1 tablespoon puréed fresh root
    ginger
4-5 tomatoes or canned
    tomatoes, drained
salt to taste
1 litre (32 fl oz) water
$\frac{1}{2}$-1 teaspoon black cummin
    seeds
a few fresh mint leaves

Preparation time: 40 minutes
Cooking time: 40 minutes

1. Wash and soak the rice for 20-30 minutes and drain. Set aside.
2. Heat the ghee or oil in a heavy-based pan and add the onions. Sauté until brown.
3. Add all the whole spices and fry for 30 seconds. Add the mushrooms, chilli powder, coriander, ginger and tomatoes and stir-fry until all the moisture has evaporated.
4. Add the drained rice and fry for a few minutes. Add the salt and the water. Bring to the boil, cover tightly and leave to simmer on a low heat until the rice is cooked and each grain is separate. Do not remove the lid for at least the first 20 minutes of cooking. Sprinkle on the cummin seeds and mint leaves.

Unsuitable for freezing.

Gucchi Pulao.

Yakhni Pulao

SERVES 4-6

Kashmiris love their rice and breads - from the most basic plain boiled rice to the exotic Biryanis and Pulaos, laced with lamb, mutton, nuts, cream and yogurt.

For the Yakhni (stock):
350g (12 oz) breast of lamb
1 teaspoon salt
1 litre (32 fl oz) water
1 small onion, chopped
2 whole cloves
3 bay leaves
12 black peppercorns

For the Pulao:
500g (1 lb) Basmati rice
1 litre (32 fl oz) water
4-5 tablespoons ghee or oil
2 medium onions, sliced
20 almonds, blanched
4 green cardamom pods
4-5 cloves garlic, peeled and
   ground to a paste
2.5cm (1 inch) piece fresh root
   ginger, peeled and ground to
   a paste
8 black peppercorns
4 whole cloves
1 blade mace, ground
1 teaspoon poppy seeds,
   ground
2.5cm (1 inch) cinnamon stick
1 teaspoon black cummin seeds
250ml (8 fl oz) natural yogurt.
salt to taste
$1/2$ teaspoon garam masala
2 tablespoons fresh mint leaves,
   chopped
2 tablespoons fresh coriander
   leaves, chopped

Preparation time: 30 minutes
Cooking time: 2 hours 30 minutes

1. Put the lamb, salt, water, onion, cloves, bay leaves and black peppercorns into a large pan. Cover and cook on a medium to low heat for 1 hour.
2. Remove the meat from the stock. There should be 1 litre (32 fl oz) of stock (yakhni). If not, add more water, bring to boiling point then strain. Remove the bones from the lamb and cut the meat into small pieces.
3. Wash the rice and soak in the water for 20 minutes.
4. Heat the ghee or oil in a heavy-based pan and add half the onion. Fry until brown and crisp. Remove from the oil. Add the almonds and fry until brown. Set aside.
5. In the same pan stir-fry the meat until brown. Remove and set aside. Fry the rest of the onion in the same ghee, adding the cardamoms, garlic and ginger pastes, peppercorns, cloves, mace, poppy seeds and cinnamon stick. Add the drained rice and continue frying for a further 5 minutes.
6. Add the meat to the rice and stir gently. Add the cummin seeds, yogurt, salt, garam masala, mint and coriander leaves and the yakhni (stock). Lower the heat. Cover tightly and leave to simmer on a low heat until the rice is cooked. Do not open the pan for the first 20 minutes of cooking. Serve garnished with the fried onions and almonds.

Suitable for freezing.

Kesar Mattar Pulao
(Saffron Peas Pulao)
SERVES 4-6

*K*ashmiris use saffron generously in their cuisine - they even flavour their tea with it. This rice dish is not only luxurious and colourful but has a delicate blend of spices and nuts to make a wonderful meal on its own or to serve with any meat, fish or vegetable.

500g (1 lb) Basmati Rice
ghee or oil
10-15 almonds, blanched and
 slivered
6-8 walnuts, shelled and
 chopped
2 tablespoons raisins
5-6 whole cloves
1-2 brown cardamom pods
2.5cm (1 inch) cinnamon stick
10-12 black peppercorns
250g (8 oz) fresh or frozen peas
$^{1}/_{2}$ teaspoon saffron, soaked in
 1 tablespoon hot water
salt to taste
600-850ml (1-1$^{1}/_{2}$ pints) water

Preparation time: 45 minutes
Cooking time: 30 minutes

1. Wash and soak the rice for 30 minutes. Drain.
2. Heat the ghee in a pan and fry the almonds, walnuts and raisins separately until the nuts become golden brown and the raisins puff up. Remove from the oil and set aside.
3. To the same ghee, add all the whole spices. Lightly fry until they change colour, stirring continuously.
4. Stir in the peas, saffron liquid, the rice and salt to taste. Fry until the rice is coated with the ghee. Add the water. Bring to the boil, reduce the heat, cover tightly and simmer for about 20 minutes or until the rice is cooked. Garnish with the fried nuts and raisins.

Suitable for freezing.

SWEETS AND
DESSERTS

Phirni
SERVES 4-6

*P*hirni is a popular Kashmiri dessert, set in 'Shikoras' and flavoured with cardamom, saffron and nuts. 'Shikoras' are traditional earthenware pots which are soaked in water for 2-3 hours so they become saturated and do not absorb any liquid from the contents. These pots are also used to set freshly prepared yogurt.

90g (3 oz) Basmati rice
water
1 litre (32 fl oz) full cream milk
125g (4 oz) sugar, or to taste
½ teaspoon saffron, soaked
  in 1 tablespoon milk
1 teaspoon ground cardamom
2 drops rose water concentrate
  or 2 teaspoons rose water
15 almonds, blanched and
  sliced
2 tablespoons shelled pistachio
  nuts, chopped
2 silver leaves for garnish
  (optional)

Preparation time: 45 minutes
Cooking time: 45-60 minutes

1. Wash the rice in cold water and leave to soak for 30 minutes. Drain and grind in a blender adding about 2-3 tablespoons water to make a fine paste.
2. Bring the milk to the boil in a heavy-based pan. Add the rice paste and sugar and whisk. Reduce the heat and continue cooking, stirring constantly to ensure that there are no lumps, until the mixture has a custard-like consistency.
3. Add the saffron and milk, cardamom and rose water concentrate or rose water. Remove the pan from the heat.
4. Pour equal quantities of the Phirni into small dessert bowls.
5. Garnish with the almonds and pistachio nuts. Leave to chill in the refrigerator. If liked, garnish with the silver leaf.

Unsuitable for freezing.

Previous pages: Zarda Pulao (p.105) and Phirni.

Zarda Pulao
(Sweet Saffron Pulao)
SERVES 4-6

*T*his recipe is evidence of the considerable influence of Persia on Kashmir. On festive occasions this pulao was used to stuff whole goats, which were then roasted on open-pit fires. Nowadays this Pulao is served on its own or with cream for a more elaborate dessert.

250g (8 oz) Basmati rice
30g (1 oz) raisins
1.5 litres (2¹/₂ pints) water
90g (3 oz) ghee or butter
6 whole cloves
8-10 green cardamom pods
30g (1 oz) shelled pistachios, sliced
30g (1 oz) almonds, blanched and slivered
150g (5 oz) sugar
250ml (8 fl oz) water
¹/₂ teaspoon saffron, soaked in 2 tablespoons hot milk
2 tablespoons kewda water
3-4 silver leaves, (optional)

Preparation time: 40 minutes
Cooking time: 45 minutes

1. Wash and soak the rice for 30 minutes. Drain and set aside.
2. Wash and soak the raisins and drain.
3. Boil the rice in 1.5 litres (2¹/₂ pints) of water and when half cooked, drain in a colander.
4. Preheat the oven to 180°C, 350°F, Gas Mark 4
5. Heat the ghee or butter in a heavy-based frying pan and add the cloves, cardamom pods, nuts, raisins, sugar, water and saffron liquid and bring to the boil. Remove from the heat.
6. Grease a casserole dish, mix together the rice and sugar mixture and add to the casserole dish. Cover the dish tightly with kitchen foil or a lid and bake in the oven for 25-30 minutes.
7. Before serving, sprinkle with kewda water and decorate with silver leaves if liked.

Unsuitable for freezing.

Khubani
(Apricot Delight)
SERVES 4-6

A dessert fit for Kings. The combination of paneer balls cooked in syrup and topped with apricots is mouth-watering. This dish is prepared at Wazawaans (celebratory banquets) and its fruity flavour is loved by all.

30 whole dried apricots
350g (12 oz) sugar
350g (12 oz) paneer
  (see page 9)
2 tablespoons arrowroot
ghee or oil for frying
500ml (16 fl oz) water
1/4 teaspoon saffron, soaked
  in 1 teaspoon water
1/2 teaspoon ground cardamom
1 teaspoon rose water

Preparation time: 20 minutes plus soaking time
Cooking time: 45 minutes

1. Soak apricots in water overnight. In the morning, add half the sugar to the soaking water and simmer the apricots until soft. Cool and gently remove the stones leaving fruit whole. Set aside.
2. Knead the paneer with the arrowroot until soft. Shape into small marble-sized balls.
3. Heat the ghee in a deep frying pan and deep-fry the balls gently until golden, on a low heat. Drain and set aside.
4. In a small pan, prepare a syrup with the remaining sugar and the 500ml (16 fl oz) of water. Bring to the boil, stirring, and cook gently until a clear syrup is formed. Add the saffron and liquid, cardamom and rose water.
5. As the syrup simmers, add the paneer balls, taking care not to break them. Cook gently until they start to look slightly translucent. Remove from the heat and cool very thoroughly.
6. Serve the paneer balls and syrup in individual bowls with a topping of apricots.

Unsuitable for freezing.

Khubani and Akroat Bharfi (p108).

Akroat Bharfi
(Walnut Sweet)
SERVES 4-6

*A*lthough the Kashmiris make only a few sweet dishes, their desserts tend to be *milk-based and rich in flavour. The full flavour of the walnuts makes this recipe a nutty delight.*

2 litres (3½ pints) full cream
  milk
300g (10 oz) sugar
500g (1 lb) shelled walnuts,
  very finely slivered or
  chopped
silver leaf (optional)

Preparation time: 10 minutes
Cooking time: 45-60 minutes

1. Grease a flat dish or baking sheet and set aside.
2. Slowly bring the milk to the boil, stirring continuously. Continue boiling gently until the milk has reduced and thickened. This process can take up to ½ hour. Add the sugar a little at a time and stir well.
3. When the sugar has dissolved, add the chopped walnuts and keep stirring on a low heat, making sure not to burn the bottom of the pan. If the milk sticks to the pan, lower the heat until the milk leaves the sides of the pan and has a dough-like consistency.
4. Spread the mixture onto the dish or baking sheet and allow to cool.
5. Apply the silver leaf if desired.
6. When cool cut into 5cm (2 inch) diamond shapes and serve.

Unsuitable for freezing.

Badam Ka Halwa
(Almond Halwa)
SERVES 4

*T*he saffron used in this recipe makes a colourful and fragrant dish that tastes as good as it smells. It is easy to prepare and makes a nice tea-time treat.

500g (1 lb) almonds
250g (8 oz) caster sugar
500ml (16 fl oz) milk
250g (8 oz) ghee or butter
15g (¹/₂ oz) green cardamom
  pods
¹/₂ teaspoon saffron, soaked in
  a little milk
2 teaspoons ground cardamom
silver leaves for garnish,
  (optional)

Preparation time: 30 minutes
Cooking time: 30 minutes

1. Soak the almonds in hot water. Drain and peel and finely grind the almonds.
2. Mix together the sugar and milk and leave the sugar to dissolve.
3. Heat the ghee in a heavy-based pan. Add the cardamom pods, and ground almonds and fry until lightly browned, stirring continuously.
4. Add the sugar-milk mixture and cook on a medium heat until the milk has reduced and the consistency is a little thicker than custard. Stir the saffron-milk and cardamom into the pan.
5. Pour into a dish and decorate with silver leaf, if liked.

Qahwa
(Kashmiri Tea)

*I*n Kashmir, drinking tea is a national pastime; it is sipped continuously throughout the day and drunk fervently after dinner.

1 litre (32 fl oz) water
1 teaspoon fresh green tea
2 small green cardamom pods,
  shelled and the seeds ground
1cm (¹/₂ inch) cinnamon stick,
  ground
5 almonds, blanched and
  shredded
6 strands saffron, crushed
sugar to taste (optional)

Preparation time: 10 minutes
Cooking time: 10-15 minutes

1. Place the water and tea leaves in a pan. Bring to the boil and then strain.
2. Put back into the pan. Add the cardamom, cinnamon, shredded almonds and saffron and continue heating. Add sugar to taste
3. Pour into individual cups and serve immediately.

Sevian Kheer
(Vermicelli pudding)
SERVES 4-6

*T*his is a very well-known dessert especially in Muslim homes where it is served during the festival of Eid. In the olden days the sevian (vermicelli) was made at home - nowadays vermicelli is commonly available in most supermarkets. Sevian is also available in a roasted form which saves time, as plain vermicelli would need to be sautéed in ghee until brown in colour.

180g (6 oz) ghee
75g (2½ oz) sevian
 (vermicelli)
1.4 litres (2½ pints) milk
10 cardamom seeds
½ teaspoon saffron, soaked in
 1 tablespoon milk
90g (3 oz) sugar or to taste
10-15 almonds, blanched and
 slivered
1 tablespoon raisins (optional)

Preparation time: 10 minutes
Cooking time: 45-60 minutes

1. Heat the ghee in a heavy-based pan and add the sevian and sauté over a medium heat, stirring gently until golden brown. Empty into a colander and allow the excess ghee to drain out. If roasted sevian is used then add directly to the milk (step 2).
2. Bring the milk to the boil in a heavy-based pan and add the sautéed or roasted sevian. Add the whole cardamom seeds and the saffron-milk and lower the heat. Simmer until the milk has been reduced by half.
3. Add the sugar, almonds and raisins and simmer for a further 5 minutes.

Serve hot or chilled.

Suitable for freezing.

Index